A NEW WINDMILL SELECTION OF
NON-FICTION

Real People,
Real Places

EDITED BY ANGELA BARRS

Heinemann Educational Publishers
Halley Court, Jordan Hill, Oxford OX2 8EJ
A division of Reed Educational and Professional Publishing Ltd

OXFORD   MADRID   ATHENS   FLORENCE
PRAGUE   CHICAGO   PORTSMOUTH NH (USA)
MEXICO CITY   SÃO PAULO   SINGAPORE
KUALA LUMPUR   TOKYO   MELBOURNE
AUCKLAND   NAIROBI   KAMPALA
IBADAN   GABORONE   JOHANNESBURG

First published in the New Windmill Series 1996

2000 99 98 97 96
10 9 8 7 6 5 4 3 2

ISBN 0 435 12448 X

British Library Cataloguing in Publication Data for this title is available from
the British Library.

Cover photographs: Bob Geldof at Live Aid concert, Frank Spooner
Pictures/Gamma (29956); Nelson Mandela on his election, Frank Spooner
Pictures/Gamma (613.994); Vera Brittain, Illustrated London News;
Zlata Filipovic, Penguin Books Ltd (Viking)

Cover design by The Point

Typeset by Books Unlimited (Nottm) NG19 7QZ

Printed and bound in the United Kingdom by Clays Ltd, St Ives plc

Contents

Introduction   i

Diaries and journals   1

Anne Frank The Diary of Anne Frank   2

Zlata Filipovic Zlata's Diary: A Child's Life in Sarajevo   13

John Smith 74 Days: An Islander's Diary of the Falklands
   Occupation   22

Beatrix Potter The Journal of Beatrix Potter 1881–1897   29

Francis Kilvert Kilvert's Diary 1870–79:
   Selections from the Diary of the Rev. Francis Kilvert   34

Biography and autobiography   39

Bob Geldof Is That It?   40

Thomas Callaghan A Lang Way to the Panshop   48

Mary Seacole Wonderful Adventures of Mrs Seacole in
   Many Lands   54

Nelson Mandela Long Walk to Freedom:
   The Autobiography of Nelson Mandela   64

Letters   73

Sarah Sarah's Letters: A Case of Shyness   74

Mark Twain Mark Twain's Letters from Hawaii   83

Angela Barrs A Letter from Jaipur   89

Edward Bawden Edward Bawden's Letters
   Home 1940–45   93

Travel   99

Ffyona Campbell On Foot through Africa   100

Eric Newby A Short Walk in the Hindu Kush   109

Christina Dodwell A Traveller in China   117

John Hillaby Journey through Europe   125

Amelia Edwards A Thousand Miles up the Nile   131

People's ideas 139

Polly Toynbee Examinations 140

Vera Brittain Keeping his Love 144

Gareth Grundy Road to Ruin 148

Neil Ascherson The English Riot 159

Activities 163

Acknowledgements 166

Introduction

Fiction is often defined in dictionaries as a 'feigned or false story' – a 'made-up' story. Non-fiction by contrast is based on fact or things that have actually happened.

'Truth' and 'fiction' are often blurred around the edges, however. Well-recognized actors from television soaps have been roundly scolded in real life for the behaviour of the characters they play in the script. Media terms like 'faction', 'docudrama' and 'news fiction' all help to blur the edges of fiction into fact. In newspapers, journalists will see the same news event from different viewpoints and then relay it to us. They will put a particular 'spin' on the story, exaggerating one angle, or omitting some facts, so that two articles about the same event appear to be very different versions of the facts. The idea that if it is in the papers then it must be true, has little to commend it.

The extracts and articles in this book record the lives and ideas of real people from the present and the past, written at home or abroad. In that sense they are true non-fiction. They represent public and private writings, from items published in magazines to those written in code or for the writer's eyes only. These women, men and young people wrote of their own experiences and reflections on the world around them, representing many cultures and periods in history.

Although the readings are grouped under separate headings to indicate what type or genre of writing they represent, a feature of this non-fiction selection is that the items often defy grouping into categories. So, for example, Mark Twain's *Letters from Hawaii* are indeed letters, but their newspaper readership makes them also entertaining journalism. Others might call them travel writing. Ffyona Campbell's *On Foot through Africa* obviously comes under the travel writing heading too, but it is the result of writing a journal of the walk and has many features of the journal or diary genre. Zlata Filipovic used Anne Frank's diary as a model for her own and so the entries look like letters … and so on.

In these pages you will read about life in other lands and times: you can see how the reality of war in different places has impacted upon real people's lives and the importance to them of writing about it; you can reflect on the ideas other people express, and measure your own opinions against theirs; you can witness how they rose to challenges and observe how they, in turn, challenge our sometimes restricted view of other people.

These writers show us black people who succeeded against extraordinary odds, the personal and public roles of eminent people, and how women as well as men have been great adventurers. Perhaps some of the most moving writing comes from young people, describing the transition from childhood to adulthood.

Each of these extracts can be read alone, or as a group under a particular genre heading. If you read in this second way you are likely to see contrasts and similarities between the extracts. This in turn may help you to understand the writer's concerns and explore how far you empathize with them.

Each section has a short introduction to the nature of the readings which follow. The information at the start of each extract tells you a little about the author or the situation in which it was written. Apart from the title of the original text from which the reading is taken, there are sometimes other titles mentioned which you might like to follow up.

In reading about real places and the people who lived in them, you will be reading non-fiction. You will be exploring people's ideas and sharing their experiences – I hope you find it an enjoyable selection.

Angela Barrs

Diaries and journals

Many of us have kept diaries or journals at various times in our lives, particularly during adolescence. Of course, many readers will consider the homework diary as one such kind of daily record, but the examples in this section do more than record details connected with daily work, however vital the diary may be for that purpose. The filofax has little room for the kind of 'thinking aloud' which is characteristic of the readings which follow.

One issue which does arise as you read these entries is – did the writer expect the diary or journal to be read by other people? (This is also an issue with letters.) Are diary and journal writers entitled to privacy, whilst they are alive, and after they are dead? Consider *The Diary of Anne Frank,* a world-famous diary, which Zlata Filipovic in the second extract knows well. It was found by Anne's father after her death and he felt he wanted it to be widely read, yet she did not write for public consumption at all. Whilst we may feel that Mr Frank provided the world with an important record in offering his daughter's diary for publication, we may not feel so sure about Beatrix Potter's journal being made available for us to read. However non-controversial her entries may seem, she chose to write in code and her editor spent much time trying to decipher it. Another famous diarist, James Boswell, was advised by his friend, the dictionary-maker Samuel Johnson, to burn his diaries in case they should fall into the wrong hands.

Three diarists in this section write about the wars they lived through. One is a middle-aged man, the others are girls who were both very young when they began their diaries. John Smith shows us the normality of his life being destroyed during the Falklands War and Zlata Filipovic tells us how it feels to live in war-torn Sarajevo. For both of these people, the place they call home is ruined and the diary seems to provide some kind of comfort for them, as did Anne Frank's, during her brief life.

1

The Diary of Anne Frank

Anne Frank

'I can shake off everything if I write; my sorrows disappear, my courage is reborn.'

Anne Frank began her diary in 1942 at the age of thirteen. She kept it faithfully for two years while she and her family lived in hiding from the Gestapo in the sealed-off back rooms of her father's office building in Amsterdam. As Jews who had fled to Holland in 1933 to escape Hitler's persecution of the Jews in Germany, the Franks were under no illusions about what would happen to them if their hiding place was discovered.

Anne, who was a lively, intelligent and sociable young teenager, must have found it hard to be cut off so completely from the outside world. She read and studied to keep herself busy, and wrote down her thoughts in her diary, which she named 'Kitty'. Anne regarded the diary as her closest friend. It became the safety-valve which enabled her to cope with the petty irritations, hunger and fear of daily life, and even to find humour and hope in her situation.

In this first extract, written before the family went into hiding, she tells her diary the story of her life so far.

Saturday, 20 June, 1942

I haven't written for a few days, because I wanted first of all to think about my diary. It's an odd idea for someone like me to keep a diary; not only because I have never done so before, but because it seems to me that neither I – nor for that matter anyone else – will be interested in the unbosomings of a thirteen-year-old schoolgirl. Still, what does that matter? I want to write, but more than that, I want to bring out all kinds of things that lie buried deep in my heart.

There is a saying that 'paper is more patient than man'; it came back to me on one of my slightly melancholy days, while I sat chin in hand, feeling too bored and limp even to make up my mind whether to go out or stay at home. Yes, there is no doubt that paper is patient and as I don't intend to show this cardboard-covered notebook, bearing the proud name of 'diary', to anyone, unless I find a real friend, boy or girl, probably nobody cares. And now I come to the root of the matter, the reason for my starting a diary: it is that I have no such real friend.

Let me put it more clearly, since no one will believe that a girl of thirteen feels herself quite alone in the world, nor is it so. I have darling parents and a sister of 16. I know about thirty people whom one might call friends – I have strings of boyfriends, anxious to catch a glimpse of me and who, failing that, peep at me through mirrors in class. I have relations, aunts and uncles, who are darlings too, a good home, no – I don't seem to lack anything. But it's the same with all my friends, just fun and games, nothing more. I can never bring myself to talk of anything outside the common round. We don't seem to be able to get any closer, that is the root of the trouble. Perhaps I lack confidence, but anyway, there it is, a stubborn fact and I don't seem to be able to do anything about it.

Hence the diary. In order to enhance in my mind's eye the picture of the friend for whom I have waited so long, I don't want to set down a series of bald facts in a diary like most people do, but I want this diary itself to be my friend, and I shall call my friend Kitty. No one will grasp what I'm talking about if I begin my letters to Kitty just out of the blue, so, albeit unwillingly, I will start by sketching in brief the story of my life.

My father was 36 when he married my mother, who was then 25. My sister Margot was born in 1926 in Frankfurt-on-Main. I followed on 12 June, 1929, and, as we are Jewish, we emigrated to Holland in 1933, where my father was appointed Managing Director of Travies N. V. This firm is in close relationship with the firm of Kolen & Co. in the same building, of which my father is a partner.

The rest of our family, however, felt the full impact of Hitler's anti-Jewish laws, so life was filled with anxiety. In 1938 after the pogroms,* my two uncles (my mother's brothers) escaped to the USA. My old grandmother came to us, she was then 73. After May, 1940, good times rapidly fled: first the war, then the capitulation, followed by the arrival of the Germans. That is when the sufferings of us Jews really began. Anti-Jewish decrees followed each other in quick succession. Jews must wear a yellow star, Jews must hand in their bicycles, Jews are banned from trams and forbidden to drive. Jews are only allowed to do their shopping between three and five o'clock and then only in shops which bear the placard 'Jewish shop'. Jews must be indoors by eight o'clock and cannot even sit in their own gardens after that hour. Jews are forbidden to visit theatres, cinemas, and other places of entertainment. Jews may not take part in public sports. Swimming baths, tennis courts, hockey fields, and other sports grounds are all prohibited to them. Jews may not visit Christians. Jews must go to Jewish schools, and many more restrictions of a similar kind.

So we could not do this and were forbidden to do that. But life went on in spite of it all. Jopie used to say to me: 'You're scared to do anything, because it may be forbidden.' Our freedom was strictly limited. Yet things were still bearable.

Granny died in January, 1942; no one will ever know how much she is present in my thoughts and how much I love her still.

In 1934 I went to school at the Montessori Kindergarten and continued there. It was at the end of the school year, I was in form 6B, when I had to say good-bye to Mrs K. We both wept, it was very sad. In 1941 I went, with my sister Margot, to the Jewish Secondary School, she into the fourth form and I into the first.

So far everything is all right with the four of us and here I come to the present day.

---

* pogroms: organized massacres

Saturday, 20 June, 1942

Dear Kitty,

I'll start straight away. It is so peaceful at the moment, Mummy and Daddy are out and Margot has gone to play ping-pong with some friends.

I've been playing ping-pong a lot myself lately. We ping-pongers are very partial to an ice-cream, especially in summer when one gets warm at the game, so we usually finish up with a visit to the nearest ice-cream shop, 'Delphi' or 'Oasis', where Jews are allowed. We've given up scrounging for extra pocket money. 'Oasis' is usually full and amongst our large circle of friends we always manage to find some kind-hearted gentleman or boyfriend, who presents us with more ice-cream than we could ever devour in a week.

I expect you will be rather surprised at the fact that I should talk of boyfriends at my age. Alas, one simply can't seem to avoid it at our school. As soon as a boy asks if he may cycle home with me and we get into conversation, nine out of ten times I can be sure that he will fall head over heels in love immediately and simply won't allow me out of his sight. After a while it cools down of course, especially as I take little notice of ardent looks and pedal blithely on.

If it gets so far that they begin about 'asking Father' I swerve slightly on my bicycle, my satchel falls, the young man is bound to get off and hand it to me, by which time I have introduced a new topic of conversation.

These are the most innocent types: you get some who blow kisses or try to get hold of your arm, but then they are definitely knocking at the wrong door. I get off my bicycle and refuse to go farther in their company, or I pretend to be insulted and tell them in no uncertain terms to clear off.

There, the foundation of our friendship is laid, till tomorrow!

Yours, Anne.

A fortnight later Anne's father tells her that the family must prepare to 'disappear' at short notice.

Sunday morning, 5 July, 1942

Dear Kitty,

Our examination results were announced in the Jewish Theatre last Friday. I couldn't have hoped for better. My report is not at all bad. I had one *vix satis*[*], a five for algebra, two sixes and the rest were all sevens or eights. They were certainly pleased at home, although over the question of marks my parents are quite different from most. They don't care a bit whether my reports are good or bad as long as I'm well and happy, and not too cheeky: then the rest will come by itself. I am just the opposite. I don't want to be a bad pupil; I should really have stayed in the seventh form in the Montessori School, but was accepted for the Jewish Secondary. When all the Jewish children had to go to Jewish schools, the headmaster took Lies and me conditionally after a bit of persuasion. He relied on us to do our best and I don't want to let him down. My sister Margot has her report too, brilliant as usual. She would move up with *cum laude*[*] if that existed at school, she is so brainy. Daddy has been at home a lot lately, as there is nothing for him to do at business; it must be rotten to feel so superfluous. Mr Koophues has taken over Travies and Mr Kraler the firm of Kolen & Co. When we walked across our little square together a few days ago, Daddy began to talk of us going into hiding. I asked him why on earth he was beginning to talk of that already. 'Yes, Anne,' he said, 'you know that we have been taking food, clothes, furniture to other people for more than a year now. We don't want our belongings to be seized by the Germans, and we certainly don't want to fall into their clutches ourselves. So we shall disappear of our own accord and not wait until they come and fetch us.'

'But Daddy, when would it be?' He spoke so seriously that I grew very anxious.

---

[*] *vix satis*: only just satisfactory   *cum laude*: with honours

'Don't you worry about it, we shall arrange everything. Make the most of your carefree young life while you can.' That was all. Oh, may the fulfilment of these sombre words remain far distant yet!

                                        Yours, Anne.

For two years the Franks depend on a few brave friends to bring them food and news of the outside world.

Friday, 9 October, 1942

Dear Kitty,

I've only got dismal and depressing news for you today. Our many Jewish friends are being taken away by the dozen. These people are treated by the Gestapo without a shred of decency, being loaded into cattle trucks and sent to Westerbork, the big Jewish camp in Drente. Westerbork sounds terrible; only one washing cubicle for a hundred people and not nearly enough lavatories. There is no separate accommodation. Men, women, and children all sleep together. One hears of frightful immorality because of this; and a lot of the women, and even girls, who stay there any length of time are expecting babies.

It is impossible to escape; most of the people in the camp are branded as inmates by their shaven heads and many also by their Jewish appearance.

If it is as bad as this in Holland whatever will it be like in the distant and barbarous regions they are sent to? We assume that most of them are murdered. The British radio speaks of their being gassed.

Perhaps that is the quickest way to die. I feel terribly upset. I couldn't tear myself away while Miep told these dreadful stories; and she herself was equally wound up for that matter. Just recently, for instance, a poor crippled Jewess was sitting on her doorstep; she had been told to wait there by the Gestapo, who had gone to fetch a car to take her away. The poor thing was terrified by the guns that were shooting at British 'planes overhead, and by the glaring beams of the searchlights. But Miep did not dare take her in; no one would undergo such a risk. The Germans strike without the slightest mercy. Elli too is very quiet: her boyfriend has got to go to Germany. She is afraid that the airmen who fly over our homes will drop their bombs, often weighing a million kilos, on Dirk's head. Jokes such as 'he's not likely to get a million' and 'it only takes one bomb' are in rather bad taste. Dirk is certainly not the only one who has to go: trainloads of boys leave daily. If they stop at a small station *en route*, sometimes some of them manage to get out unnoticed and escape; perhaps a few manage it. This, however, is not the end of my bad news. Have you ever heard of hostages? That's the latest thing in penalties for sabotage. Can you imagine anything so dreadful?

Prominent citizens – innocent people – are thrown into prison to await their fate. If the saboteur can't be traced, the Gestapo simply put about five hostages against the wall. Announcements of their deaths appear in the papers frequently. These outrages are described as 'fatal accidents'. Nice people, the Germans! To think that I was once one of them too! No, Hitler took away our nationality long ago. In fact, Germans and Jews are the greatest enemies in the world.

Yours, Anne.

The hiding-place is shared with another family – the Van Daans and their teenage son Peter. The confined space and lack of privacy often lead to friction. Anne recognizes the need for positive thinking, as this extract shows.

Tuesday, 10 August, 1943

Dear Kitty,
New idea. I talk more to myself than to the others at mealtimes, which is to be recommended for two reasons. Firstly, because everyone is happy if I don't chatter the whole time, and secondly, I needn't get annoyed about other people's opinions. I don't think my opinions are stupid and the others do; so it is better to keep them to

myself. I do just the same if I have to eat something I can't stand. I put my plate in front of me, pretend that it is something delicious, look at it as little as possible and before I know where I am, it is gone. When I get up in the morning, also a very unpleasant process, I jump out of bed thinking to myself, 'You'll be back in a second', go to the window, take down the black-out, sniff at the crack of the window until I feel a bit of fresh air, and I'm awake. The bed is turned down as quickly as possible, and then the temptation is removed. Do you know what Mummy calls this sort of thing? 'The Art of Living' – that's an odd expression. For the last week we've all been in a bit of a muddle about time, because our dear and beloved Westertoren clock bell has apparently been taken away for war purposes, so that neither by day nor night do we ever know the exact time. I still have some hope that they will think up a substitute (tin, copper or some such thing) to remind the neighbourhood of the clock.

Whether I'm upstairs or down, or wherever I am, my feet are the admiration of all, glittering in a pair of (for these days) exceptionally fine shoes. Miep managed to get hold of them second-hand for Fl.27.10, wine-coloured suède leather with fairly high wedge heels. I feel as if I'm on stilts and look much taller than I am.

Dussel has indirectly endangered our lives. He actually let Miep bring a forbidden book for him, one which abuses Mussolini and Hitler. On the way she happened to be run into by an SS car. She lost her temper, shouted 'Miserable wretches', and rode on. It is better not to think of what might have happened if she had had to go to their headquarters.

Yours, Anne.

Anne begins to fall in love with Peter Van Daan.

Thursday, 6 January, 1944

Dear Kitty,

My longing to talk to someone became so intense that somehow or other I took it in my head to choose Peter.

Sometimes if I've been upstairs into Peter's room during the day, it always struck me as very snug, but because Peter is so retiring and would never turn anyone out who became a nuisance, I never dared stay long, because I was afraid he might think me a bore. I tried to think of an excuse to stay in his room and get him talking, without it being too noticeable, and my chance came yesterday. Peter has a mania for crossword puzzles at the moment and hardly does anything else. I helped him with them and we soon sat opposite each other at his little table, he on the chair and me on the divan.

It gave me a queer feeling each time I looked into his deep blue eyes, and he sat there with that mysterious laugh playing round the lips. I was able to read his inward thoughts. I could see on his face that look of helplessness and uncertainty as to how to behave, and, at the same time, a trace of his sense of manhood. I noticed his shy manner and it made me feel very gentle; I couldn't refrain from meeting those dark eyes again and again, and with my whole heart I almost beseeched him: oh, tell me, what is going on inside you, oh, can't you look beyond this ridiculous chatter?

But the evening passed and nothing happened, except that I told him about blushing – naturally not what I have written, but just so that he would become more sure of himself as he grew older.

When I lay in bed and thought over the whole situation, I found it far from encouraging, and the idea that I should beg for Peter's patronage was simply repellent. One can do a lot to satisfy one's longings, which certainly sticks out in my case, for I have made up my mind to go and sit with Peter more often and to get him talking somehow or other.

Whatever you do, don't think I'm in love with Peter – not a bit of it! If the Van Daans had had a daughter instead of a son, I should have tried to make friends with her too.

I woke at about five to seven this morning and knew at once, quite positively, what I had dreamt. I sat on a chair and opposite me sat Peter ... Wessel. We were looking together at a book of drawings by Mary Bos. The dream was so vivid that I can still partly remember the drawings. But that was not all – the dream went on. Suddenly Peter's eyes met mine and I looked into those fine, velvet brown eyes for a long time. Then Peter said very softly, 'If I had only known I would have come to you long before!' I turned round brusquely because the emotion was too much for me. And after that I felt a soft, and oh, such a cool kind cheek against mine and it felt so good, so good ...

I awoke at this point, while I could still feel his cheek against mine and felt his brown eyes looking deep into my heart, so deep, that there he read how much I had loved him and how much I still love him. Tears sprang into my eyes once more, and I was very sad that I had lost him again, but at the same time glad because it made me feel quite certain that Peter was still the chosen one.

It is strange that I should often see such vivid images in my dreams here. First I saw Grandma[*] so clearly one night that I could even distinguish her thick, soft, wrinkled velvety skin. Then Granny[*] appeared as a guardian angel; then followed Lies, who seems to be a symbol to me of the suffering of all my girlfriends and all Jews. When I pray for her, I pray for all Jews and all those in need. And now Peter, my darling Peter – never before have I had such a clear picture of him in my mind. I don't need a photo of him, I can see him before my eyes, and oh, so well!

Yours, Anne.

---

[*] Grandma is grandmother on Father's side, Granny on Mother's side.

In August 1944 the hiding-place was discovered by the Gestapo and the Frank and Van Daan families were sent to concentration camps in Poland and Germany. Anne and her sister Margot died in Bergen-Belsen early in 1945, a few weeks short of Anne's sixteenth birthday. Her diary was found in the hiding-place by Miep, who kept it and gave it to Mr Frank when the war ended.

Zlata's Diary: A Child's Life in Sarajevo

Zlata Filipovic

This diary was written by a person even younger than Anne Frank. Zlata Filipovic, Fipa to her friends, began the diary whilst confined to the family flat, during the war in the former Yugoslavia. She was eleven when she began writing and finally left Sarajevo with her parents just before Christmas 1993 for a safer life in France. From what she writes, it is clear that she gained comfort from writing her diary, even whilst shells dropped around her in Sarajevo.

As you read her diary, you feel time pass, even though Zlata does not write each day. Her pet canary and a stray cat help her to retain some kind of routine during the war, through caring for them. Her diary-writing does this too. She notes how the passing months are affecting her parents: 'They don't look like my old Mummy and Daddy any more.' She only realizes how time has passed when she finds her clothes have become too small for her.

Although she is too young for secondary school at the time these particular diary entries were written, she is old enough to know that she cannot understand why her city is being bombed. She speaks of the politicians who give orders for battle as 'kids'. For her, these adults are playing games with people's lives.

Zlata knew why Anne Frank, hidden in a Dutch attic from the Nazis, felt her diary was a close friend. For Anne Frank, for Zlata, and John Smith, the middle-aged diarist whose writing you can read after Zlata's, keeping a diary during wartime was a way of keeping a hold on normality.

Zlata holding her diary

Monday, 30 March 1992

Hey, Diary! You know what I think? Since Anne Frank called her diary Kitty, maybe I could give you a name too. What about:

ASFALTINA	PIDŽAMETA
ŠEFIKA	HIKMETA
ŠEVALA	MIMMY

or something else???
　I'm thinking, thinking …
　I've decided! I'm going to call you
　MIMMY
　All right, then, let's start.

Dear Mimmy,
It's almost half-term. We're all studying for our tests. Tomorrow we're supposed to go to a classical music concert at the Skenderija Hall. Our teacher says we shouldn't go because there will be 10,000 people, pardon me, children, there, and somebody might take us as hostages or plant a bomb in the concert hall. Mummy says I shouldn't go. So I won't.
　Hey! You know who won the Yugovision Song Contest?! EXTRA NENA!!!???
　I'm afraid to say this next thing. Melica says she heard at the hairdresser's that on Saturday, 4 April 1992, there's going to be BOOM-BOOM, BANG-BANG, CRASH Sarajevo. Translation: they're going to bomb Sarajevo.

Love,
Zlata

Friday, 3 April 1992

Dear Mimmy,
Mummy is at work. Daddy has gone to Zenica. I'm home from school and have been thinking. Azra leaves for Austria today. She's afraid of war. HEY! Still, I keep thinking about what Melica heard at the hairdresser's.

What do I do if they bomb Sarajevo? Safia is here, and I'm listening to Radio-M. I feel safer.

Mummy says that what Melica heard at the hairdresser's is misinformation. I hope so!

Daddy came back from Zenica all upset. He says there are terrible crowds at the train and bus stations. People are leaving Sarajevo. Sad scenes. They're the people who believe the misinformation. Mothers and children are leaving, the fathers are staying behind, or just children are leaving, while their parents stay. Everybody is in tears. Daddy says he wishes he hadn't seen that.

Love you, Mimmy,
Zlata

Saturday, 4 April 1992

Today is Bairam.* There aren't many people in the streets. I guess it's fear of the stories about Sarajevo being bombed. But there's no bombing. It looks as though Mummy was right when she said it was all misinformation. Thank God!

Love you,
Zlata

Sunday, 5 April 1992

Dear Mimmy,

I'm trying to concentrate so I can do my homework (reading), but I simply can't. Something is going on in town. You can hear gunfire from the hills. Columns of people are spreading out from Dobrinja. They're trying to stop something, but they themselves don't know what. You can simply feel that something is coming, something very bad. On TV I see people in front of the B-H parliament building. The radio keeps playing the same song: 'Sarajevo, My Love'. That's all very nice, but my stomach is still in knots and I can't concentrate on my homework any more.

Mimmy, I'm afraid of WAR!!!

Zlata

* Bairam: a Muslim religious festival

Monday, 6 April 1992

Dear Mimmy,
Yesterday the people in front of the parliament tried peacefully to cross the Vrbanja bridge. But they were shot at. Who? How? Why? A girl, a medical student from Dubrovnik, was KILLED. Her blood spilled onto the bridge. In her final moments all she said was: 'Is this Sarajevo?' HORRIBLE, HORRIBLE, HORRIBLE!

NO ONE AND NOTHING HERE IS NORMAL!

The Baščaršija has been destroyed! Those 'fine gentlemen' from Pale fired on Baščaršija!

Since yesterday people have been inside the B-H parliament. Some of them are standing outside, in front of it. We've moved my television set into the living room, so I watch Channel 1 on one TV and Good Vibrations on the other. Now they're shooting from the Holiday Inn, killing people in front of the parliament. And Bokica is there with Vanja and Andrej. Oh, God!

Maybe we'll go to the cellar. You, Mimmy, will go with me, of course. I'm desperate. The people in front of the parliament are desperate too. Mimmy, war is here. PEACE, NOW!

They say they're going to attack RTV Sarajevo.* But they haven't. They've stopped shooting in our neighbourhood. KNOCK! KNOCK! (I'm knocking on wood for good luck.)

WHEW! That was close. Oh, God! They're shooting again!!!

Zlata

Thursday, 9 April 1992

Dear Mimmy,
I'm not going to school. All the schools in Sarajevo are closed. There's danger hiding in these hills above Sarajevo. But I think things are slowly calming down. The heavy shelling and explosions have stopped. There's occasional gunfire, but it quickly falls silent. Mummy and Daddy

* RTV Sarajevo: the radio and TV centre

aren't going to work. They're buying food in huge quantities. Just in case, I guess. God forbid!

Still, it's very tense. Mummy is beside herself, Daddy tries to calm her down. Mummy has long conversations on the phone. She calls, other people call, the phone is in constant use.

Zlata

Sunday, 12 April 1992

Dear Mimmy,

The new sections of town – Dobrinja, Mojmilo, Vojničko polje – are being badly shelled. Everything is being destroyed, burned, the people are in shelters. Here in the middle of town, where we live, it's different. It's quiet. People go out. It was a nice warm spring day today. We went out too. Vaso Miskin Street was full of people, children. It looked like a peace march. People came out to be together, they don't want war. They want to live and enjoy themselves the way they used to. That's only natural, isn't it? Who likes or wants war, when it's the worst thing in the world?

I keep thinking about the march I joined today. It's bigger and stronger than war. That's why it will win. The people must be the ones to win, not the war, because war has nothing to do with humanity. War is something inhuman.

Zlata

Tuesday, 14 April 1992

Dear Mimmy,

People are leaving Sarajevo. The airport, train and bus stations are packed. I saw sad pictures on TV of people parting. Families, friends separating. Some are leaving, others staying. It's so sad. Why? These people and children aren't guilty of anything. Keka and Braco came early this morning. They're in the kitchen with Mummy and Daddy, whispering. Keka and Mummy are crying. I don't think they know what to do – whether to stay or to go. Neither way is good.

Zlata

Wednesday, 15 April 1992

Dear Mimmy,

There has been terrible gunfire in Mojmilo. Mirna spent a whole 48 hours in the shelter. I talked to her on the phone, but not for long because she had to go back down to the shelter. I feel sorry for her.

Bojana and Verica are going to England. Oga is going to Italy. And worst of all, Martina and Matea have already left. They went to Ohrid*. Keka is crying, Braco is crying and Mummy is crying. She's on the phone right now, and she's crying. And 'those boys' up there in the hills keep shooting at us. I just heard that Dejan has left too.

OOOHHHHH! Why war?!

Love you, Mimmy,
Zlata

Thursday, 16 April 1992

Dear Mimmy,

Martina, Matea and Dejan didn't leave, after all. That's really not fair! Yes, of course it is, they mustn't go. But it isn't fair because we all cried our eyes out and in the end they didn't leave. There are not enough buses, trains or planes for all the people who want to get out of here.

Love you,
Zlata

Saturday, 18 April 1992

Dear Mimmy,

There's shooting, shells are falling. This really is WAR. Mummy and Daddy are worried, they sit up until late at night, talking. They're wondering what to do, but it's hard to know. Whether to leave and split up, or stay here together. Keka wants to take me to Ohrid. Mummy can't make up her mind – she's constantly in tears. She tries to hide it from me, but I see everything. I see that things aren't good here. There's no peace. War has suddenly

---

* Ohrid: a lakeside town in Macedonia

entered our town, our homes, our thoughts, our lives. It's terrible.

It's also terrible that Mummy has packed my suitcase.

Love,
Zlata

Monday, 20 April 1992

Dear Mimmy

War is no joke, it seems. It destroys, kills, burns, separates, brings unhappiness. Terrible shells fell today on Baščaršija, the old town centre. Terrible explosions. We went down into the cellar, the cold, dark, revolting cellar. And ours isn't even all that safe. Mummy, Daddy and I just stood there, holding on to each other in a corner which looked safe. Standing there in the dark, in the warmth of my parents' arms, I thought about leaving Sarajevo. Everybody is thinking about it, and so am I. I couldn't bear to go alone, to leave behind Mummy and Daddy, Grandma and Grandad. And going with just Mummy isn't any good either. The best would be for all three of us to go. But Daddy can't! So I've decided we should stay here together. Tomorrow I'll tell Keka that you have to be brave and stay with those you love and those who love you. I can't leave my parents, and I don't like the other idea of leaving my father behind alone either.

Your Zlata

Tuesday, 21 April 1992

Dear Mimmy,

It's horrible in Sarajevo today. Shells falling, people and children getting killed, shooting. We will probably spend the night in the cellar. Since ours isn't safe, we're going to our neighbours, the Bobars. The Bobar family consists of Grandma Mira, Auntie Boda, Uncle Žika (her husband), Maja and Bojana. When the shooting gets bad, Žika phones us and then we run across the yard, over the ladder and the table, into their building and finally knock at their door. Until just the other day we took the street, but there's shooting and it's not safe any more. I'm getting ready to go to the cellar. I've packed my backpack with biscuits, juice, a deck of cards and a few other 'things'. I can still hear the cannon fire, and something that sounds like it.

Love you, Mimmy,
Zlata

Wednesday, 22 April 1992

Dear Mimmy,
We spent the whole night in the Bobars' cellar. We went there at around 21.30 and came home at about 10.30 the next morning. I slept from 4.00 to 9.30am. It boomed and shook really badly last night.

Zlata

Sunday, 26 April 1992

Dear Mimmy,
We spent Thursday night with the Bobars again. The next day we had no electricity. We had no bread, so for the first time in her life Mummy baked some. She was scared how it would turn out. It turned out like bread – good bread. That was the day I was supposed to go to Ohrid with M&M. But I didn't, and neither did they.
Ciao!

Your Zlata

Tuesday, 28 April 1992

Dear Mimmy,
SNIFFLE! Martina, SNIFFLE, and Matea, SNIFFLE, left YESTERDAAAY! They left by bus for Krško.[*] They went with Keka. Oga has gone too, so has Dejan, Mirna will be leaving tomorrow or the next day, and soon Marijana will be going too.
SNIFFLE!
Everybody has gone. I'm left with no friends.

Zlata

* Krško: a town in Slovenia

74 Days: An Islander's Diary of the Falklands Occupation

John Smith

John Smith went to live in the Falkland Islands in 1958, working on a research ship. Then, as now, the islands were British, although they lie very close to the south-eastern tip of Argentina. He married Ileen, who was born in the Falklands, and they had four children, Jeremy, Martyn, Anya and Tyssen. In 1982, Argentina challenged the British right to the Falklands and invaded the islands with a large occupation force. Argentina surrendered, but only after 74 days and many casualties.

Many British soldiers, sailors and air-crew died during the conflict but many more Argentines died on the islands. The average age of the Argentine soldiers, John Smith thought, was seventeen and most of them were conscripted. He believed them to be untrained and called them 'cannon fodder'. It appears that many of them died through malnutrition and exhaustion as well as by direct fire. In this first brief glimpse of life under occupation, John Smith shows the absurd nature of the war situation.

Friday 21 May – Day Fifty

Ileen, Anya and Jeannie have been busy preparing food all day, ready for a possible extended stay in the bunker. The boys and I continued to build the fence in the back garden. The Argentines have put four of their helicopters in the shelter of the rocky ridge over at the Camber, well camouflaged, but the rotor blades glint in the sun which rather gives them away.

Towards the end of Mass this afternoon, we heard the sound of a jet aircraft overhead with no firing breaking out, so assumed that it was an Argentine. Afterwards, while outside on the steps, there was a great burst of firing from the airport, with clouds of black smoke. An Argentine TV crew were filming it from the back of the town hall. We heard later that they had shot down one of their own planes and then opened fire on the helicopter which had gone off to rescue the pilot. They are getting rather jumpy.

Late this afternoon we suddenly discovered that we had an Argentine soldier stationed outside the house, apparently some sort of guard, done up like a miniature arsenal with pistol, rifle and grenades. This was not really on, so invited him in for a cup of coffee. He was a bit hesitant at first, but a plate of cakes went a long way in helping him to make up his mind. He didn't speak a great deal of English, but we were able to have sort of a fractured conversation, during which he told us that all was well with his army; everything was going fine; no problems. We were not entirely convinced. He stayed for nearly an hour, then somewhat furtively took up his position outside the gate again. We had thought of offering him a cigarette, but he would have gone up like a Brocks[*] benefit night with all that weaponry strung about him.

I think that the Argentines may be keeping an eye on us, as so many young people, especially lads between eighteen and twenty, come to the house during the afternoons. They may suspect that there is some sort of subversive movement being set up. They do seem very afraid of this sort of thing. We do, I suppose, look a bit suspicious, for besides Jeremy, Martyn and Rag who are permanent, there are also Peter Roberts, Graham Bound, Ramon Miranda, Cousin Zachary, etc., who all pop in for a beer, cup of tea or a chat and also to pinch whatever cakes or buns may be lying about.

The diary continues, with entries of various lengths, until the last days of occupation, which are described in some detail.

---

[*] Brocks: firework manufacturer who supplied charity displays

Sunday 13 June – Day Seventy-three

A cold, bright day with very high cloud; a light covering of snow on the ground. Wind west, Force 2–3.

Had a remarkably good sleep, the best for many weeks, although there was apparently continuous heavy firing through the night. The first I heard of it was at 7.40 this morning when I woke up.

It's been a day of non-stop intense firing from all sides. According to one news broadcast, this is the heaviest artillery exchange and bombardment since World War II. They are quoting incredible numbers of shells having been fired during the past few hours, running into many thousands. (That's only from the British side; the Argentines are sending over thousands in return.)

A great umbrella of shells is now over Stanley, being fired non-stop in three directions: by the Argentines, outwards towards the advancing British Army in the mountains; from the British Army, which is firing on the Argentine positions; and from the Royal Navy, who are pounding the southern perimeter of the town from the sea. Overhead the Harriers ceaselessly pound the Argentine positions, with cannon fire and bombs. It is impossible adequately to describe the noise, which is now almost constant. The air is filled with the stinging smell of cordite. Every few minutes the Argentine fire their 155mm monsters from up at the back of the town. These guns don't go bang, they bark with a deep twanging crack, which grates on one's nerves after a while. Our house, and I suppose everyone else's, shakes and shudders continually. If we hadn't taken the pictures down the other day they would certainly have fallen down today. Besides the bangs, we have the whistles as the shells fly overhead, then the crash of the explosions, deafening ones from the British shells as they land on the Argentine positions, and distant crumps as the Argentine shells land in the mountains. By the look of it they are using a lot of air burst, which can plainly be seen in the crisp, still air. Possibly the noise is even more intense today, as there is not sufficient wind to carry it away. Stanley is circled by erupting earth, smoke

British troops in the Falkland Islands, 1982

and flames. The Argentine army is trapped, beneath this torrent of unrelenting fire – so are we.

About 11.30 this morning poor old Wilfred Newman's house up on Davis Street received a direct hit and burned to the ground very quickly in a great mass of smoke and flames. The British are obviously trying to hit the Argentine 155mm that is between the houses up there. Another shell went through the roof of Harry Milne's garage, in which he had all the new furniture for his house stored. Another damaged Bob Stewart's and Derek Evans' house. From here it looked very much as though Pat and Maureen's house had gone up, so Jeremy went up on to the roof with the binoculars to see what was happening. It was impossible to see accurately which house had been hit, as Wilfred's was next door to Pat's. Two Argentine military police then arrived, saying that looking through binoculars was not allowed. They insisted on going upstairs to see how he had managed to get on to the roof, then they wanted to confiscate the binoculars, but fortunately their attention was distracted by something else being hit close by, so they went off in a hurry. Blast them and their stupid regulations. Something big has just gone up at the back of the new hostel; masses of black smoke and flames high into the air. I think an Argentine helicopter may have received a direct hit.

Just after lunch – which none of us had, or even thought about – Nidge Buckett brought old Fred Coleman down to stay with us. Up until this morning he had refused to budge from his house, but had to be forcibly removed as it was getting so dangerous up there on Davis Street. He's well into his eighties and very deaf and was most apologetic that they had not allowed him the time to change before bringing him down. He did, however, manage to grab his best cap, put an overcoat over the top of his pyjamas and bring a bottle of rum. We soon had him settled in front of the fire with a hot rum and his carpet slippers, watching the television. He had not seen television before and was most impressed, saying that he was unable to hear a thing but enjoyed the pictures. He looked so splendid and comfortable sat there among the chaos of the sitting-room.

It's surprising that they have managed to keep the television going under such frightening conditions.

We are now all of us feeling the strain of things, even the boys. Ileen is bearing up wonderfully well. Surely it can't get much worse than this. It was perhaps a stupid thing to do, but we all went to Mass this afternoon, trying to carry on as normally as possible. It was rather noisy but the volume of the responses was in accordance with the volume of the gunfire. The church creaked and swayed a lot.

Walking back towards home afterwards was a sad, uncanny experience. In the cold, through the mud and the slush in the pale, wintry sunshine of late afternoon. The noise of the Argentine guns seemed louder, as more and more they were being drawn in towards the town. Their smoke created a haze in the air; their smell stung our eyes and our throats. The British guns on the mountains pounded on relentlessly as they advanced inexorably towards Stanley. It was difficult to grasp that all this was happening in our once serene and tranquil Stanley. It was like having a nightmare – sitting on the outside of a situation looking in, paralyzed, unable to do anything whatsoever to stop this awful holocaust which hourly is increasing in its violence, so that soon it must explode in a great fury all around us.

Despite the tension, life still goes on. The Ashworth family still deliver the milk whatever the discomforts. Dennis Place and his lads from the filtration plant are still out dodging shells in their efforts to keep the fresh water supply flowing. The hospital and its staff are prepared for whatever may come. Les Biggs and Chris McCallum are still working every daylight hour assisting the old and the infirm to places of safety. Duffy and Nidge Buckett are doing the same thing, as, no doubt, are many others in the town. It is difficult to know, as we are restricted very much to our own parts of Stanley. People are still able to raise a hopeful smile. Late this afternoon one of the Harriers dropped a green flare over the town; could this be significant?

At curfew this evening we were able to see the Royal Marines barracks at Moody Brook still blazing. It's been on fire for most of the day; there seems to be very little left now. The garage at the hospital has been cleared out during the day to accommodate more Argentine wounded. The Beaver hangar is said to be a mortuary, with hundreds of Argentine bodies in it. Today's icy conditions have caused several more spectacular disasters among the military vehicles. Many are in unusual positions on the hills and in gardens. The shaking and vibration today has been too much for our lovely Wedgwood carving dish; the inner section has split into two pieces. A great shame as it was over 150 years old.

The Journal of Beatrix Potter 1881–1897

Beatrix Potter

Beatrix Potter is widely known because of her illustrated stories of animals, written for children. They have been translated into many languages, and the pictures she drew are to be found on china, calendars and tea towels. Her house, Hill Top, in the Lake District has become a museum and an attraction for international tourists, yet in her lifetime, she was an extremely private person. The journal she kept for sixteen years is an example of this, for she wrote in code so automatically that it was as easy for her to use as ordinary script.

In 1913, she married William Heelis, and from then on developed another role as Mrs Heelis, a knowledgeable sheep farmer. With the money from her children's books Beatrix Potter bought property and land which was bequeathed to the National Trust, and we benefit from her foresight and generosity when visiting the Lake District landscape which she helped to protect.

Her early life was rather dull, except for family holidays. When she visited places like Falmouth in Cornwall, her journal begins to record what was for her a great change in lifestyle. Reading it today, it tells of a part of Britain untouched by industrialization and full of surprises for Beatrix. Falmouth, at the time she wrote, was a thriving port with ships trading from many countries. If we consider the very long journey from London to Falmouth by train which the Potter family made, we may be less surprised by her remarks about people's physical appearances. For her the holiday was to foreign parts like a 'long-haul' flight is for us.

This is a quiet, well-conducted town, which is the more remarkable owing to the number of British and foreign seamen loitering about. It forms a great contrast to the

Devonshire towns, particularly Ilfracombe, but it may be
the Welsh who upset the latter place.

I have seen only one man drunk since we have been here,
and observed no fighting or roughness of any sort amongst
the sailors. They loll about in the main street, spitting on
the pavement, their only objectionable habit; shake hands
with one another in an elaborate manner, and stare
unmercifully for the first week. Indeed all the people do
that, and appear inquisitive, and if you look back they pass
the time of day amiably.

The foreign sailors stare impartially at everything in a
fidgety inquisitive fashion. Some of them are very
picturesque. I saw one leaning against a post on the quay
for hours, in a scarlet woollen cap, bright blue jersey, and
great sea-boots, others with sashes round their middles,
and one old Frenchman in sabots. They appear on their
good behaviour and attract no attention amongst the
natives.

The town is cosmopolitan, one sees five languages on the
window of the barber's shop. Everything has a nautical
flavour, the baker sells *ship bread*, the grocer calls himself
a ship's chandler, the ironmonger's window is full of
binnacles, pulleys and lanterns, sail cloth is the leading
article at the drapers, and in one shop they announce fresh
water on sale. Also, every mortal shop sells Valencia
oranges, such bad ones too.

It is a poor town for shops, except one or two connected
with the shipping, and the streets very narrow and steep.
They are not over-clean either, and in the morning every
householder sets out a pail or wooden box of refuse, right
out on the pavement, and there is a smell of rotten fish.

Burton's old curiosity shop which makes the greatest
display is quite a museum, crammed from floor to garret
with odds and ends, but the great part absolute rubbish.
The foreign things, which form the greater part of the stock,
struck me as not so much bona-fide curios bought from
sailors, as an inferior class or article imported wholesale.
Perhaps the oddest part of this collection was a great
quantity of French cavalry sabres, pistols, helmets and
bayonets from German battlefields and the surrender of Metz.

How he got them I know not, but they were certainly genuine, any quantity of sabres at five shillings apiece and holster pistols, said to be Waterloo, and rusty enough for Blenheim, at about the same price. There were hideous African idols and weapons labelled 'poisoned' in large letters, which is a novel way of attracting purchasers, but indeed it seemed more of a museum than a shop.

Mr Burton, a stout grey gentleman in spectacles reading a paper would hardly answer enquiries lest he should appear to press one, and his trust and confidence were really charming. Ladies and gentlemen were requested to walk up into twelve rooms including the garrets, and on the stairs tumble over several large ships' bells which they may ring if they want an attendant.

Little Miss Burton, who explained from a long way off that I had not broken some dancing Japanese pottery, which was true, but she could not possibly see. I bought a white pot-head of bone which was one of the few English curios of any antiquity, excepting a man-trap and sundry small cannon-balls.

* * *

As to [Mr Burton's] trust and confidence, I fancy it is justified by the conduct of the town. There are three policemen – I have seen one of them at the Barbers. They have a Hutch no larger than the Tub of Diogenes[*], at the back of Custom House Quay, with a great flag-staff and a very little garden.

They are the most odd specimens, just ordinary natives dressed up in blue clothes, and all seem to have bunions, or very mis-fitting boots. They are on friendly conversational terms with the other sailors, and I have seen one of them having eggs at a Butchers.

The people here are all singularly alike, and one can well believe the statement that they are the purest bred race in Britain. I am only surprised that the old Cornish dialect has died out earlier than several others, for they are

---

[*] Diogenes: the Greek philosopher who believed the human race did not need luxury and demonstrated this by living in an old barrel

extremely isolated in situation, and if one or two persons whom I have talked to were fair examples, they are naive and unspoiled to an amusing degree. Very friendly, kindly, cheerful, healthy, long-lived, and the numerous old people very merry, which speaks well for a race.

The children are extremely pretty, but like the Welsh, it goes off. The women certainly are not on the whole, though intelligent and fresh-complexioned. The universal type is black or rusty, with crisp hair, women more black than men, and blue eyes very common with both shades.

An ordinary type with the men, (the young men especially, are so like as to be twins), is short thick neck, slump in the chops, short straight nose, (with the women very commonly turns up, which is a reason why they are the less good looking), and in both sexes a straight narrow forehead, eyebrows strongly marked and deep-set.

As the men's faces become thinner through age, it is apparent that they have high cheek-bones. I notice with the red type, the nose is occasionally less straight, but always short. The women have singularly oval faces.

The town men, though their hair is very strong, are neatly trimmed. Our driver has a head like a dagger, (he was particularly Cornish, very civil, but with a certain naive dignity or reserve. I was shocked to discover that this man was Scotch), but the quarry-men and farm-labourers look veritable ancient Britons, with their wild black locks and light blue eyes. All the same I fancy they are very mild.

* * *

One thing that lends animation to this town is the presence of the *Ganges*[*] boys. Lads mostly between fifteen and seventeen, from the training ship *Ganges,* which is moored high up in the Carrick Roads[*]. They are sent here when first recruited, bag rag and bob-tail, to learn the first rudiments of drill and discipline, (there are only dummy guns on board), and their spirits can really be only compared to ginger beer. They are somewhat noisy but

---

[*] *Ganges*: permanently moored as a naval training base for boys
Carrick Roads: the inlet to the east of Falmouth

always in charge of a superior officer when on shore, and their healthiness and clean merry faces make them a pleasure to look at.

My father was photographing at Mylor, where there is a naval yard or store. A boatload of these boys arrived at the quay, and having spied him, they began to whistle and arranged themselves in an elaborate group. He took off his hat to them when he had finished, and to his surprise and confusion they raised a cheer.

They look the picture of health, but I am surprised to hear there have been one or two epidemics of diphtheria on the *Ganges*. Perhaps it is too full, 500 on board, and it is not large for an old three-decker. It looks beautifully clean, and a little garden in one of the galleries at the stern. They set the sails occasionally, but the ship has only twice been moved from her moorings in the last twenty years.

Possibly the diphtheria may come in with some fresh boy, but it is mysterious how epidemics can spread, even in this pure air, (though it occurs to me that may account for it, I never observed such an air for transmitting smells). They have had influenza very generally at Lizard Town, which is separated from every where by ten miles of moor.

Kilvert's Diary 1870–79: Selections from the Diary of the Rev. Francis Kilvert

Francis Kilvert

Francis Kilvert lived during the reign of Queen Victoria and, despite being a poor clergyman, he devoted himself to his work and to enjoying life in a way which made his parishioners love him. These entries are taken from his diary kept during the winter of 1870–71, which seems to have been most severe. He was working as curate to the vicar of Clyro in the Wye Valley and his diary gives such a happy account of his time in the district that admiring readers began to call the area 'Kilvert Country' and to visit the places he described.

Just as Beatrix Potter makes the town of Falmouth come alive to readers, so Francis Kilvert takes us back to a time before central heating when people not only skated on ice but danced formal quadrilles, such as the Lancers and the Sir Roger de Coverley, on it.

In the final entry here, Francis Kilvert's brother Edward, known to his family as Teddy or Perch, seems to have taken offence at a friend outside the family using his nickname. Not even the skater losing his balance seems to have restored his sense of humour. His brother records it all and contrasts this light-hearted scene with some grisly facts about the icy weather.

Sunday, Christmas Day

As I lay awake praying in the early morning I thought I heard a sound of distant bells. It was an intense frost. I sat down in my bath upon a sheet of thick ice which broke in the middle into large pieces whilst sharp points and jagged edges stuck all round the sides of the tub like *chevaux de frise*,* not particularly comforting to the naked thighs and loins, for the keen ice cut like broken glass. The

---

* *chevaux de frise*: military defences with spikes

ice water stung and scorched like fire. I had to collect the floating pieces of ice and pile them on a chair before I could use the sponge and then I had to thaw the sponge in my hands for it was a mass of ice. The morning was most brilliant. Walked to the Sunday School with Gibbins and the road sparkled with millions of rainbows, the seven colours gleaming in every glittering point of hoar frost. The Church was very cold in spite of two roaring stove fires. Mr V preached and went to Bettws.

Monday, 26 December

Much warmer and almost a thaw. Left Clyro at 11am.

At Chippenham my father and John were on the platform. After dinner we opened a hamper of game sent by the Venables, and found in it a pheasant, a hare, a brace of rabbits, a brace of woodcocks, and a turkey. Just like them, and their constant kindness.

Tuesday, 27 December

After dinner drove into Chippenham with Perch and bought a pair of skates at Benk's for 17/6. Across the fields to the Draycot water and the young Awdry ladies chaffed me about my new skates. I had not been on skates since I was here last, five years ago, and was very awkward for the first ten minutes, but the knack soon came again. There was a distinguished company on the ice, Lady Dangan, Lord and Lady Royston and Lord George Paget all skating. Also Lord and Lady Sydney and a Mr Calcroft, whom they all of course called the Hangman. I had the honour of being knocked down by Lord Royston, who was coming round suddenly on the outside edge. A large fire of logs burning within an enclosure of wattled hurdles. Harriet Awdry skated beautifully and jumped over a half sunken punt. Arthur Law skating jumped over a chair on its legs.

Wednesday, 28 December

An inch of snow fell last night and as we walked to Draycot to skate the snow storm began again. As we passed Langley Burrell Church we heard the strains of the quadrille band

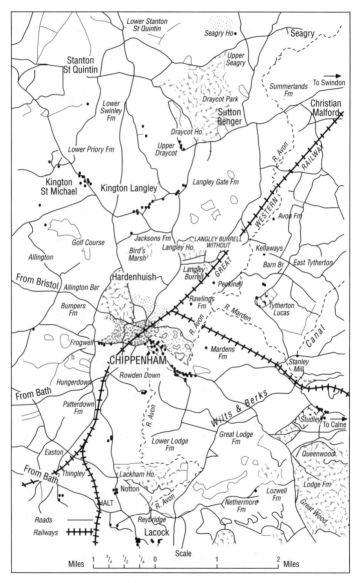

Chippenham and district

on the ice at Draycot. The afternoon grew murky and when
we began to skate the air was thick with falling snow. But
it soon stopped and gangs of labourers were at work
immediately sweeping away the new fallen snow and skate
cuttings of ice. The Lancers was beautifully skated. When
it grew dark the ice was lighted with Chinese lanterns, and
the intense glare of blue, green, and crimson lights and
magnesium riband made the whole place as light as day.
Then people skated with torches.

New Year's Day, 1871

My mother, Perch and I sat up last night to watch the old
year out and the New Year in. The wind was in the North
and the sound of the bells came faintly and muffled over the
snow from Chippenham and Kington. We opened the
dining room window to 'loose in' the sound of the chimes
and 'the New Year' as they say in Wales. It was bitter cold,
but we went to the door, Perch and I, to hear better. I was
carrying my travelling clock in my hand and as we stood on
the terrace just outside the front door, the little clock struck
midnight with its tinkling silvery bell in the keen frost. We
thought we could hear three peals of Church bells,
Chippenham, St Paul's, and very faintly Kington. 'Ring
happy bells across the snow.'

When Perch came back from skating at Draycot last
night, he amused us with an account of Friday's and
Saturday's doings on the ice. On Friday they had a
quadrille band from Malmesbury, skated quadrilles,
Lancers, and Sir Roger de Coverley. Then they skated up
and down with torches, ladies and gentlemen pairing off
and skating arm in arm, each with a torch. There were
numbers of Chinese lanterns all round the water, blue,
crimson and green lights, magnesium riband, and a fire
balloon was sent up. Maria Awdry, forgetting herself and
the passage of time, inadvertently spoke to Perch calling
him 'Teddy' instead of 'Mr Kilvert'. Having done which she
perceived her mistake, turned 'away and smote herself on
the mouth', while Perch 'looked at her with a face like a
stone'. While people were standing about in groups or

skating up and down gently young Spencer skated up suddenly with outstretched arm to shake hands with Teddy. At the critical moment his skate hitched and he lost his balance and made a deep but involuntary obeisance before Perch, describing 'an attenuated arch', with his fingers and toes resting on the ice. People hid their faces, turned and skated away with a sour smile or grinning with repressed laughter. Perch stood still waiting for the 'attenuated arch' to unbind itself and retrieve its erect posture, 'looking on with a face like a stone'. Gradually the 'arch' rose from its deep obeisance. The arch was the arch described by an attenuated tom cat. During the torch skating Harriet Awdry hurled her half-burnt torch ashore. Lord Cowley was walking up and down the path on the bank watching with great impatience the skaters whom he detests. The fiery torch came whirling and flaming through the dark and hit the noble diplomatist sharply across the shins, rebounding from which it lay blazing at the foot of a tree. Lord Cowley was very angry. 'I wish these people wouldn't throw their torches about here at me,' grumbled his lordship. 'Come away and hide behind the island or he'll see you,' said Perch to Harriet. So they glided away and from the cover of the island they watched Lord Cowley angrily beating the blazing torch against the ground to try to put it out. But the more he beat it, the more the torch flamed and showered sparks into his face. Harriet described the incident thus, 'I hit old Cowley such a crack over the shins.'

Last week Mr Greenwood, the Calne organist, fell on the Bowood ice and broke his nose. The next day his son, a boy of 15, fell while sliding, struck his head against a stone, fractured his skull and died in an hour and a half by the lake side.

Biography and autobiography

There is a sense in which all writing is really autobiography: if we use our experience to write with, then our lives are what we use. Biographers too write about people who have held a personal fascination for them, a particular interest which links in with the biographer's own life.

The writing of biography and autobiography is a way of remaking life-stories, and telling them in the way we want them to be. Mary Seacole, whose story is told in this section, was famous in her own lifetime, but with the passage of time is now famous only amongst those working in the field of nursing today. In her own life, lived in several different continents, she featured in newspaper articles as an example of bravery and dedication.

Nelson Mandela's autobiography opens with a description of his rural upbringing and a village life of such simplicity that it is remarkable he has risen from obscurity, through long imprisonment, to lead his country out of the years of apartheid. Fame does not necessarily endure, and 'Saint Bob', who tells of bringing Band Aid to starving Ethiopia in the second extract, may already be slipping away from media attention.

Geldof made us re-think our attitudes to food and with today's consciousness about healthy eating you may be amused or horrified by how public health was once ignored in Thomas Callaghan's experience. As a delivery boy first for a grocer and then for a butcher, Callaghan tells us what it was like to grow up in poverty in the 1930s.

The life stories in this section are created versions of people's lives because total recall is not possible and the writers select and reconstruct the past. They tell us a great deal about the place and time in which these people lived. People's choices are affected by the places and times they live in. Reading other people's stories may allow you to reflect on your own life experience by comparing the choices they made with those you face yourself.

Is That It?

Bob Geldof

In Chapter 13 of his autobiography, Bob Geldof writes of turning on the television news one evening towards the end of 1984 and seeing 'something that placed my (financial) worries in a ghastly new perspective. The news report was of famine in Ethiopia.' He says that the newscaster's tone revealed the enormity of the horror. At the time, Geldof was a musician with Boomtown Rats, but the following day he suggested to friends that a record should be made and its sales go to benefit the starving Ethiopians.

It seemed that musicians everywhere were thinking along these lines but Geldof was the one who took the idea seriously, first talking to Midge Ure, then Sting, Simon le Bon, Spandau Ballet and many others. Not only individual musicians but record companies, music stores, newspapers and television gave support to what became Band Aid. In the end, the song 'Do They Know It's Christmas?' raised several million pounds to provide life-saving food and earned Geldof the name 'Saint Bob'.

For Midge it had been a day of professional triumph to produce his greatest contemporaries singing and playing on a song he'd co-written. Trevor Horn, the owner of the studio and one of Britain's greatest producers, had come in late in the evening and coached the singers through the rest of the song. Sting had gone home, thinking he was finished, and when I rang him, he travelled without complaint back across London with his girlfriend and kid. It felt good, it felt like it should. It sounds corny, but they had trusted me, now I was determined I would do my best for them.

I left the studio and went straight to the BBC to offer an exclusive play of the tape to Radio One. 'I want you to play this record. I want you to play it all the time,' I said to the producer at the BBC.

'Thanks, we'll look at it and if it's good it will get the same treatment as any record.'

'No. This is not just any record. It is a way of helping to stop people from dying. You don't play this because it is a good record. You play this because it is your way of helping. Everyone has to do what they can. We make records, that's our job: we've made this. You play records, that's your job: you play this, that's how you help. Sting said, "You have to give of yourself." That's how you do it.' He thought I was a pious, over-the-top twat.

Before Simon Bates played it I explained to the listeners, 'First you will hear Paul Young, then Boy George, then …' and I ended by saying, 'Virtually one hundred per cent of the money from this record, apart from the VAT, goes straight to Band Aid and I swear every penny will get to Ethiopia. I want everyone listening to buy it. We've only got three weeks. Let's make it the biggest selling record of all time. Paul McCartney's 'Mull of Kintyre' sold about two and a half million and that's the biggest so far. But there's fifty-six million people in this country. So we can easily beat that. Even if you've never bought a record in your life before, get it. It's only £1.30. That's how cheap it is to give someone the ultimate Christmas gift – their life. It's pathetic, but the price of a life this year is a piece of plastic with a hole in the middle.'

I began a round of TV, radio, and newspaper interviews. The mouth that had got me into trouble so often now talked about the simple idea of personal responsibility. The thing I first groped with back in the Simon Community in Dublin now became clear, 'Everyone can do something. No matter what you do, you can do something. Use your talent, your circumstances, anything. There are millions dying in agony. How many more children will you let die in your living rooms before you act? You can do something, and please buy this record. Buy one for each of your family. If you have no money, club together and buy one. Even if you hate the song, buy it and throw it away.'

The idea caught the imagination of the public and the media too, who began to catalogue the innumerable bizarre ways in which people were responding. People were buying boxes of the record and sending them out as Christmas cards. Others walked in, bought 50, kept one, and then gave the other 49 back for re-sale. A butcher in Plymouth rang me to ask if you needed special permission to sell records. When I said no, he got rid of all the meat from his window and filled it with the record. The Queen's grocer, Fortnum and Mason, phoned to ask for two boxes to sell in their restaurant; by the end they had sold thousands there.

It was impossible, during the very first few days of sale, for the record to register in that week's charts as these had already been compiled. When we tried to get the video on *Top of the Pops*, I was horrified to find that the producer, Michael Hurll, who is possibly by default the most powerful man in the British music industry, refused to include it on the grounds that the programme's policy was that only records already in the charts should be played. There were no special cases, he said. Not even for eight million people at risk of dying. Learning the lesson from Maxwell and the *Mirror* I went straight to the top. I went to the BBC reception desk and asked to be put through to the controller of BBC1, Michael Grade. He told me to send up the video which we had had made of the recording session. It was a brilliant piece of work by Nigel Dick who had assembled the crew and equipment and filmed, processed and edited it for free. He had it ready in an unprecedented 48 hours. The video perfectly captured the emotion of the day.

I waited in the BBC lobby for five minutes, and then I rang Michael. 'Have you seen it yet?' 'Yes it's brilliant. What's the problem?'

I explained about *Top of the Pops*, but suggested we had our own little five-minute programme possibly getting David Bowie to introduce the video. This would, in fact, be better than actually being on *Top of the Pops*. I waited in the lobby half an hour, then I spoke to Michael again.

'Fine,' he said. 'I've shifted the programmes here by about five minutes just before *Top of the Pops*.'

This was incredible. We would be listed in the papers as a TV programme. Millions would watch. We were slotted between the news and *Top of the Pops* – giving us a massive captive audience. As I'd hoped everything about this record was proving superlative.

At Number One that week was a singer called Jim Diamond who had never had a hit record before. I heard him interviewed about his success and he said, 'I'm delighted to be Number One, but next week I don't want people to buy my record, I want them to buy Band Aid instead.' I couldn't believe it. As a singer who hadn't had a Number One for five years, I knew what it cost him to say that. He had just thrown away his first hit for others. It was genuinely selfless. The next week 'Do They Know It's Christmas?' went straight in at Number One. That was the kind of generosity of spirit which was abroad.

The record was a phenomenon. We were printing 320,000 copies a day and still it wasn't enough. Every record factory in Britain, Ireland and Europe was pressing it. The T-shirts which we had franchised out to make even more money could not be made quickly enough, and when pirates started bringing out counterfeit merchandise we got the breakfast TV programmes to track them down. The indignation of the public and the ruthless exposure stopped that quickly.

Things began to blur. It was like the first experience of coming from Ireland to England and entering the pop world, but this time the driving force was outside rather than inside me. There seemed a different point to this, a point which was undeniable.

I flew to the States. Already the record was massive out there too. But I had had less time to concentrate on America, unsure as I was four weeks previously whether we'd even have a record in England. We only had a total of ten days' sale in the US before Christmas. I went to make those ten days as productive as possible. Will there be an American Band Aid? they asked. It was not impossible, I told them, but it was up to the American bands to organize it, not me. I was willing to help and give advice.

That night I called Cindi Lauper, the Cars, Hall and Oates, all of whom said they'd love to do a record. But my own priorities had to be the Band Aid record, and in the meantime people in the States could buy the British record.

'Do They Know It's Christmas?' sold a million and a half copies in the US in two weeks. Ironically it never got to Number One although it was outselling the actual Number One by 400 per cent, because the American charts are based on a ludicrous combination of factors of which sales are only a part. Moreover we did not get the same co-operation that we got in Britain. I suspected many retailers did not report record sales because it was not in their interest to have a non-profit making record at Number One during their peak period. I rang *Billboard* to accuse them of graft. How could we possibly outsell the Number One record four to one and not be Number One? 'It doesn't work like that, Bob.' 'Obviously not,' I thought.

No one had had the chance to do any accounting yet but already it was quite clear that we had raised around two or three million pounds. One night I sat at home listening to carol singers outside on the street. They were singing 'Silent Night'. Then they began to sing 'Do They Know It's Christmas?'. I was by myself so I cried. On Christmas Day on *Top of the Pops* the Band Aid team got together and sang it prior to the Queen's Speech to the Commonwealth.

I had assumed that soon after Christmas it would all be over. Midge was in the middle of making an album and went back to it. The Rats had a tour lined up to promote *In the Long Grass*. I had decided against releasing the LP halfway through December as planned, fearing that people might think that the whole of Band Aid was a publicity stunt for the record. In fact, of course, it was the opposite. While people were playing 'Do They Know It's Christmas?', no one thought of playing 'Dave'. I could understand this, but I was saddened to think that 'Dave' had missed its time. Our tour was a success, but the album, released in the dead period of early January, was a failure, as we knew in our hearts it would be. The music press predictably had now begun to attack the band on the grounds that Band Aid had been a Geldof gimmick.

But the national press didn't. The whole Band Aid phenomenon was manifestly too huge and too deep to be so reduced. Indeed they fanned the issue.

'When are you going to Ethiopia to see for yourself, Bob?' they kept asking. I knew why. It would be a good story: the pop star and the starving child in the same photograph. That was precisely why I had no intention of going. 'It is not necessary. I don't need to go there to see it. I've seen it already on television. There are experts to help decide how best to spend the money. They don't need a half-assed pop singer. Can't you see how distasteful that would be?' But taste never having been one of the strong points of the British popular press, this point seemed to elude them.

There was a man called Peter Searle who kept phoning me too. He said he was from a charity called World Vision.

'I don't know why you're ringing. I'm not able to distribute any money.'

'We don't want any money. We just think you should go and see the problem. We can organize a flight for you and we have a plane in Ethiopia.'

I was very suspicious. I had never heard of World Vision. Then I was told they were an excellent organization but with roots in the right-wing American evangelical revival. Later we backed several of their projects.

I was rapidly learning more about the problems of Ethiopia and its hapless peoples, caught between the millstones of natural disaster and international politics. I was finding out about the imbalance which characterizes the relationship between ourselves and the poor of the Third World. The United Nations' children's fund, Unicef, had sent their resident representative in Addis Ababa to give me a detailed briefing on the situation. Even Searle, who continued to call with his requests that I should visit one of his projects and thereby draw attention to it, was giving me useful information about the place.

Record sales had now put five million pounds in Band Aid's bank account. The problem now was what to do with that money. Nearly every agency I'd talked to would have had to take part of the money to cover their colossal overheads. These are necessary when organizations are permanent, and require a large staff if they are to function properly. But I had given my word that a hundred per cent of every penny would go to Africa without being side-tracked or wasted. If someone gave a pound, then a pound would go. The only way around the problem was to eliminate the middleman and go direct to the source. That meant going to Addis Ababa, the capital of Ethiopia. I also felt that as the money came from all over the world, no agency from a single nation should have access to it.

But how was I to decide who got what? Equally, if we did not simply hand over the money, how was *I* to order grain, charter planes and ships, fill out order sheets, custom forms, bills of lading, and so on. Band Aid was me, Philip Rusted, the accountant who had agreed to look after the money, and the lawyer John Kennedy, the last two recruited by Midge's manager Chris Morrison. 'I think you'd better go,' he said. 'At least find out what they want.'

I capitulated. I had no money to get there and I was determined that I was not touching one penny of what had been given. All I could do was get those who had insisted I went to pay. The *Daily Star* covered my hotel bills in Ethiopia and the breakfast television station, TV AM, paid for my flight. In the end they did not accompany me because of the small-minded and mercenary attitude of the television unions who scuppered all coverage, insisting it was a documentary story, not a news story which only required half the number of film crew. I found this unbelievable. The *Daily Express* were to pay my hotels in the Sudan.

Before we went I talked to the papers and TV stations concerned. I said there must be no pictures of me with starving children. They said I was being unreasonable. I said, 'Fine. I have to go: I have no money myself. I cannot spend Band Aid money, but I will get there and you won't be with me.' I didn't want it to be an exclusive story, because that would have been shabby, selling something so awful for the price of a ticket. Everyone had given money, everyone deserved to know where it was going, everyone was involved, there could be no exclusives on Band Aid. They finally agreed and they still paid my bills. The *Daily Star* tried to book every seat on the flight to Addis, but were told to shove it. In the event the flight out to Addis had a heavy quota of television and newspaper journalists from other organizations. We had not been in the air long when I felt a tap on my shoulder. I turned to see a large, ruddy-faced avuncular character who extended his hand and said with a smug smile, 'Bob, Peter Searle, World Vision.'

A Lang Way to the Panshop

Thomas Callaghan

Thomas Callaghan grew up in Newcastle upon Tyne in the 1930s. His family was amongst the poorest of the poor in Newcastle's West End. In his autobiography *A Lang* [Long] *Way to the Panshop* [Pawnshop] he tells of sharing a big double bed in a two-room flat with his father and three older brothers, of what it was like to be desperately hungry, and of pawning clothes to stave off hunger pangs. Thomas' early world was very tough, but he also paints a rich portrait of people with a lively sense of humour and a fighting spirit.

In the world of the permanently unemployed, Thomas quickly learned to fend for himself. The following extracts tell of his early experiences in the world of work.

When the school broke up for the summer holidays in 1938, the day I thought I had been yearning for arrived. I was fourteen years old and now I was free at last from the tyranny of the wasteful elementary education machine.

Of course, had I been aware as to what my future hardships and prospects were to be, I would have begged my father and my headmaster to allow me to remain at school, secure in that haven of make-believe.

Now in place of summer weeks of freedom to play at cowboys on Geordie Goddards field, or on the quarry behind the Grand cinema, in the face of stiff competition I had to seek full-time work!

To my often previous requests that I be given the opportunity of wearing long trousers, the reply from my father had always been: 'When you leave school son.' Well, I had left school, and I was excited that I would have a pair of long trousers in time to seek work on the Monday. To my horror on the Saturday evening I witnessed my mother cutting down and altering a pair of my father's work-day trousers. Growing up or not, I went to bed weeping.

On the Monday, dressed in my father's rejected trousers, I left the house to begin my quest for work. I am sure there couldn't have been a more self-conscious creature on earth that morning. I was aware of the many amused glances being cast on me from the neighbours standing in the street, but it was left to the kids who were gathered there, as though expecting to witness some ridiculous spectacle, to loudly proclaim how I looked, and indeed how I felt: 'Hey Tommy – you've got yer fathers troosers on – what a bloody mess yer look.' For the first time since I could remember, I galloped down the street and I was not pretending to be one of my favourite western heroes on his horse. I was simply running away out of sight.

After a thorough search I eventually observed a card in a grocer's shop window advertising for a 'Smart Strong Errand-Boy'. Without a moment's hesitation I entered the shop and applied for the job. I informed the manager that I was one of the strongest and fastest kids in the neighbourhood. With unemployment being so high, I was obviously determined to impress the manager. I succeeded for he offered me the job.

The very next morning in the shop the manager convinced me that he had believed me quite sincerely the day before when I had boasted about my strength. He ordered me to go out into the backyard and take out the carrier cycle into the lane where it could be loaded up with grocery orders. Whoever invented the commercial carrier cycle may have been a clever sort of man. However, when I set eyes upon the machine that I was expected to use I was of the immediate opinion that whoever had built this ugly huge machine ought to have kept it for his own use, or presented it to some industrial museum. Although it was a machine of uncertain age, mainly kept together by numerous bindings of old wire, I was convinced it would have even been a cycle difficult to manoeuvre from the day it had been manufactured.

The manager and his assistant came out into the lane, as I was placing the bike up on its stand. 'Get up on to the bike,' said the manager, 'and we'll load up the carrier for you.' So I climbed up on to the seat and I mean climb! When

I was sitting on it my toes just about reached the pedals. Both of them began packing parcels into the large carrier basket; the assistant manager, a young good-looking chap, tried not to fill the basket too much, but in vain. So I mildly remarked that I would have to be able to see where I was going, which would be difficult if they piled up the packages any higher.

'Well, Tich,' said the dry-looking unhumorous manager, after placing the last order on top, 'they're all for Pendower estate.' And with his foot, he kicked up the cycle stand into the clips that secured it. Instantly, the back wheel lifted up in the fashion of a playful horse objecting to the weight of its rider. The packages flew in all directions. Fortunately for me, I went only in one direction and in one piece, and escaped with nothing but a bruised knee. I was thankful to survive this unprovoked assassination attempt by this grocer-manager, but I decided I would have to watch him carefully in the future.

I suggested to the manager that he allow me to decide what weight I could handle with safety for, as I pointed out, as I was a quick walker and a fast runner, it should be obvious I would be a swift cyclist. He reluctantly agreed to my proposal.

However, I must state this was the first time on any cycle in my life and I wish to take this opportunity to warn any prospective errand-boy not to attempt to learn the skill of cycling on a carrier-bike, especially when it's loaded with merchandise, and the machine is perhaps held together by wire salvaged from Danish egg boxes.

'Keep looking straight ahead, Son, and keep your eyes off the front wheel,' were the parting words of the assistant manager. I learned later that it was sound advice; but at that particular time his counsel had me concerned no-end, for any minute on my travels I was expecting the front wheel to drop off. However, as I was cycling up Pendower Way, it was the chain that fell off, in two pieces! In twenty minutes, I proved to myself that I probably possessed some mechanical skill by fixing it.

On Tyneside in winter, one can always rely on experiencing a fair amount of Eskimo scenery, and so when the snow lay too deep for cycling then I had to load up the large clumsy delivery barrow, which ran on heavy wheels encircled with a metal rim, and haul it along the terrace and up steep hills, real heavy work. Even the many cart horses that passed me on my travels usually jerked their heads around to stare at me in surprise even though they themselves were working every bit as hard as myself.

After a few more jobs, including working on a building site, Thomas was once again looking for work.

The following week I became a butcher's errand boy. No time wasted with me when it came to wage earning and helping to make ends meet.

Within two hours of being shown the know-how, I was making sausages like an expert; whether they were fit for human consumption is another matter! My new employer was a one-man firm, and he informed me at the beginning he had to be able to rely on his errand boy being swift and quick-witted. Well, I was of the opinion that no errand boy was swifter than myself, and he soon taught me what being quick-witted meant, in his terms. From the worn-out fridge, he brought out two large enamel dishes of seedy looking meat scraps, and a small dish of sausage skins, which were green in colour instead of being white. Handing me an empty lemonade bottle and threepence, he directed me to go the chemist along the road and purchase threepenneth of 'Doctor'. On the way, I had it in the back of my mind that the boss was perhaps no different from the leg-pullers on the building sites, and was deliberately sending me on a fool's errand. If so, I was not complaining, it was his pay-time that was being wasted not mine. But at the chemist's the assistant took my bottle went behind the prescription partition, and soon returned with my bottle two-thirds full of a colourless liquid resembling water. On my return to the shop, the boss poured a small amount of this liquid over the sausage skins; in about five minutes those skins were bleached white. One dish of the meat scraps was put through the mincer, then he sprinkled a fair amount of the 'Doctor' over it, and to my amazement, the meat took on a natural healthy colour – and it smelt fresh too. Following his instructions I took over the operation, added the other usual ingredients, being a little heavy-handed on the seasoning, mixed it up into a dough, and then through the sausage machine it went. That liquid was not called 'Doctor' for nothing; it certainly gave the Harley Street treatment to the sausage meat. But young as I was then, I would not have fed a stray cat on the finished product.

Next, my boss instructed me on how to make potted meat. In the back-shop there was an old boiler, similar to the type found in many of the backyards of the district, and used by the tenants to do their washing in. I cut up the scraps of meat from the second container, poured some 'Doctor' over it, and tipped the lot into the boiler.

It is surprising what cooking will conceal to some degree. After less than two hours boiling, the boss declared that the meat was cooked. I scooped this mess out and filled up a number of small enamel dishes. After cooling them I placed them all in the fridge, such as it was.

The next morning, these dishes of meat were placed in the window, with a card displaying in large bold letters, 'Freshly Made Potted Meat'.

If anyone reading this assumes that the meat-treatment I have described above was solely the speciality of this one-man firm, let me state that a few months later I was employed as an errand-boy at a branch of one of the largest chain-butchers in the country, and the same unappetizing methods were practised there also. One must remember, in many of the shops in those days, refrigeration was often in a backward state. Nevertheless nothing whatsoever was wasted in the butchering trade and Monday morning was the obvious day for any weekend waste to be processed.

I gathered early on that my boss was just about scraping through financially on a week-to-week basis. To his credit, he never kept me over my hours, nor did he ever rob me of a half-day holiday.

Within a few weeks of Britain declaring war, about two-thirds of my employer's customers departed into the

countryside in order to escape from the possible risk of
air-raids. The result of this sudden exodus decided him that
he had no alternative but to close up shop.

Wonderful Adventures of Mrs Seacole in Many Lands

Mary Seacole

History has a strange way of remembering some people and forgetting others, even though they were famous in their day. Mary Seacole travelled the world as a doctor. She provided treatment in a cholera epidemic in her home town of Kingston, Jamaica, and worked on the Crimean battlefields. Florence Nightingale is, of course, very famous for caring for wounded soldiers of the Crimean War. Both women were equally famous in their own day, but Seacole is little known today, perhaps because of prejudice against her as a black woman.

Attitudes to race are reflections of society just as much then as now. Seacole was of mixed race but particularly proud of her Scottish ancestry and, as these extracts show, was intolerant of some other races. If her views of other races make uneasy reading today, they might not have seemed so surprising then.

In other ways, she was an unusual person for her times, braving public disapproval to travel as a lone, black woman in Europe and the Near East. Despite her offers to provide medical assistance alongside Nightingale, the British government did not respond and she financed herself to travel to the Crimean war zone where she was looked upon as a mother by the soldiers she treated.

In the first extract from her autobiography, she is on her way to help with the wounded but stops to meet Florence Nightingale.

We stopped at Malta also, where, of course, I landed, and stared about me, and submitted to be robbed by the lazy Maltese with all a traveller's resignation. Here, also, I met friends – some medical officers who had known me in Kingston; and one of them, Dr F, gave me a letter of introduction to Miss Nightingale.

The interior of Mrs Seacole's Crimean hotel

So on, past beautiful islands and shores, until we are
steaming against a swift current, and an adverse wind,
between two tower-crested promontories of rock, which
they tell me stand in Europe and in Asia, and are connected
with some pretty tale of love in days long gone by. Ah!
travel where a woman may, in the New World or the Old,
she meets this old, old tale everywhere. It is the one bond
of sympathy which I have found existing in three quarters
of the world alike. So on, until the cable rattles over the
windlass, as the good ship's anchor plunges down fathoms
deep into the blue waters of the Bosphorus – her voyage
ended.

I do not think that Constantinople impressed me so much
as I had expected. The caicques* might be made more safe
and commodious for stout ladies, even if the process
interfered a little with their ornament. Time and trouble
combined have left me with a well-filled-out, portly frame
– the envy of many an angular Yankee female – and, more
than once, it was in no slight danger of becoming too
intimately acquainted with the temperature of the
Bosphorus. But I will do the Turkish boatmen the justice to
say that they were as politely careful of my safety as their
astonishment and regard for the well-being of their
caicques (which they appear to love as an Arab does his
horse, or an Esquimaux his dogs, and for the same reason
perhaps) would admit. Somewhat surprised, also, seemed
the cunning-eyed Greeks, who throng the streets of Pera,
at the unprotected Creole woman who took Constantinople
so coolly (it would require something more to surprise her);
while the grave English raised their eyebrows
wonderingly, and the more vivacious French shrugged
their pliant shoulders into the strangest contortions. I
accepted it all as a compliment to a stout female tourist,
neatly dressed in a red or yellow dress, a plain shawl of
some other colour, and a simple straw wide-awake, with
bright red streamers. I flatter myself that I woke up sundry
sleepy-eyed Turks, who seemed to think that the great

---

* caicques: light Turkish rowboats

object of life was to avoid showing surprise at anything; while the Turkish women gathered around me, and jabbered about me, in the most flattering manner.

I found time, before I left the 'Hollander', to charter a crazy caicque, to carry me to Scutari, intending to present Dr F's letter to Miss Nightingale.

It was afternoon when the boatmen set me down in safety at the landing-place of Scutari, and I walked up the slight ascent, to the great dull-looking hospital. Thinking of the many noble fellows who had been borne, or had painfully crept along this path, only to die within that dreary building, I felt rather dull. As soon as I entered the hospital, and came upon the long wards of sufferers lying there so quiet and still, a rush of tears came to my eyes, and blotted out the sight for a few minutes. But I soon felt at home, and looked about me with great interest. The men there were, many of them, very quiet. Some of the convalescent formed themselves into little groups around one who read a newspaper; others had books in their hands, or by their side, where they had fallen when slumber overtook the readers, while hospital orderlies moved to and fro, and now and then the female nurses, in their quiet uniform, passed noiselessly on some mission of kindness.

I was fortunate enough to find an old acquaintance, who accompanied me through the wards. This was an old 97th man – a Sergeant T, whom I had known in Kingston, and who was slowly recovering from an attack of dysentery, and making himself of use here until the doctors should let him go back and have another 'shy at the Rooshians'. He is very glad to meet me, and tells me his history very socially, and takes me to the bedside of some comrades, who had also known me at Up-Park Camp. My poor fellows! how their eyes glisten when they light upon an old friend's face in Turkish barracks – put to so sad a use, three thousand miles from home. Here is one of them – 'hurt in the trenches,' says the Sergeant, with shaven bandaged head, and bright, restless, Irish eyes, who hallooes out, 'Mother Seacole! Mother Seacole!' in such an excited tone of voice; and when he has shaken hands a score of times, falls back upon his pillow very wearily. But I sit by his side, and try to cheer him with talk about the future, when he shall grow well, and see home, and hear them all thank him for what he has been helping to do, so that he grows all right in a few minutes; but, hearing that I am on the way to the front, gets excited again; for, you see, illness and weakness make these strong men as children, not least in the patient unmurmuring resignation with which they suffer. I think my Irish friend had an indistinct idea of a 'muddle' somewhere, which had kept him for weeks on salt meat and biscuit, until it gave him the 'scurvy', for he is very anxious that I should take over plenty of vegetables, of every sort. 'And, oh! mother!' – and it is strange to hear his almost plaintive tone as he urges this – 'take them plenty of eggs, mother; we never saw eggs over there.'

At some slight risk of giving offence, I cannot resist the temptation of lending a helping hand here and there – replacing a slipped bandage, or easing a stiff one. But I do not think anyone was offended; and one doctor, who had with some surprise and, at first, alarm on his face, watched me replace a bandage, which was giving pain, said, very kindly, when I had finished, 'Thank you, ma'am.'

One thought never left my mind as I walked through the fearful miles of suffering in that great hospital. If it is so here, what must it not be at the scene of war – on the spot where the poor fellows are stricken down by pestilence or Russian bullets, and days and nights of agony must be passed before a woman's hand can dress their wounds. And I felt happy in the conviction that *I must* be useful three or four days nearer to their pressing wants than this.[*]

It was growing late before I felt tired, or thought of leaving Scutari, and Dr S, another Jamaica friend, who had kindly borne me company for the last half-hour, agreed with me that the caicque was not the safest conveyance by night on the Bosphorus, and recommended me to present my letter to Miss Nightingale, and perhaps a lodging for the night could be found for me. So, still under the

---

[*] In fact it often took longer than four days to convey the sick and wounded from the battlefields and camps in the Crimea, across the Black Sea to Scutari where the main hospitals were situated

Sergeant's patient guidance, we thread our way through passages and corridors, all used as sick-wards, until we reach the corner tower of the building, in which are the nurses' quarters.

I think Mrs B, who saw me, felt more surprise than she could politely show (I never found women so quick to understand me as the men) when I handed her Dr F''s kind letter respecting me, and apologized for troubling Miss Nightingale. There is that in the Doctor's letter (he had been much at Scutari) which prevents my request being refused, and I am asked to wait until Miss Nightingale, whose every moment is valuable, can see me. Meanwhile Mrs B questions me very kindly but with the same look of curiosity and surprise.

What object has Mrs Seacole in coming out? This is the purport of her questions. And I say, frankly, to be of use somewhere; for other considerations I had not, until necessity forced them upon me. Willingly, had they accepted me, I would have worked for the wounded, in return for bread and water. I fancy Mrs B thought that I sought for employment at Scutari, for she said, very kindly –

'Miss Nightingale has the entire management of our hospital staff, but I do not think that any vacancy –'

'Excuse me, ma'am,' I interrupt her with, 'but I am bound for the front in a few days;' and my questioner leaves me, more surprised than ever. The room I waited in was used as a kitchen. Upon the stoves were cans of soup, broth, and arrowroot, while nurses passed in and out with noiseless tread and subdued manner. I thought many of them had that strange expression of the eyes which those who have gazed long on scenes of woe or horror seldom lose.

In half an hour's time I am admitted to Miss Nightingale's presence. A slight figure, in the nurses' dress; with a pale, gentle, and withal firm face, resting lightly in the palm of one white hand, while the other supports the elbow – a position which gives to her countenance a keen inquiring expression, which is rather marked. Standing thus in repose, and yet keenly observant – the greatest sign of impatience at any time a slight, perhaps unwitting motion of the firmly planted right foot – was Florence Nightingale[*] – that English woman whose name shall never die, but sound like music on the lips of British men until the hour of doom.

She has read Dr F's letter, which lies on the table by her side, and asks, in her gentle but eminently practical and business-like way, 'What do you want, Mrs Seacole – anything that we can do for you? If it lies in my power, I shall be very happy.'

So I tell her of my dread of the night journey by caicque, and the improbability of my finding the 'Hollander' in the dark; and, with some diffidence, threw myself upon the hospitality of Scutari, offering to nurse the sick for the night. Now unfortunately, for many reasons, room even for one in Scutari Hospital was at that time no easy matter to find; but at last a bed was discovered to be unoccupied at the hospital washerwomen's quarters.

My experience of washerwomen, all the world over, is the same – that they are kind soft-hearted folks. Possibly the soap-suds they almost live in find their way into their hearts and tempers, and soften them. This Scutari washerwoman is no exception to the rule, and welcomes me most heartily. With her, also, are some invalid nurses; and after they have gone to bed, we spend some hours of the night talking over our adventures, and giving one another scraps of our respective biographies. I hadn't long retired to my couch before I wished most heartily that we had continued our chat; for unbidden and most unwelcome companions took the washerwoman's place, and persisted not only in dividing my bed, but my plump person also. Upon my word, I believe the fleas are the only industrious creatures in all Turkey. Some of their relatives would seem to have migrated into Russia; for I found them in the Crimea equally prosperous and ubiquitous.

In the morning, a breakfast is sent to my mangled remains, and a kind message from Mrs B, having reference

* Subsequently I saw much of Miss Nightingale, at Balaclava

to how I spent the night. And, after an interview with some other medical men, whose acquaintance I had made in Jamaica, I shake hands with the soft-hearted washerwoman, up to her shoulders in soap-suds already, and start for the 'Hollander.'

In the second extract, Mary Seacole tells briefly of her war work.

But the reader must not forget that all this time, although there might be only a few short and sullen roars of the great guns by day, few nights passed without some fighting in the trenches; and very often the news of the morning would be that one or other of those I knew had fallen. These tidings often saddened me, and when I awoke in the night and heard the thunder of the guns fiercer than usual, I have quite dreaded the dawn which might usher in bad news.

The deaths in the trenches touched me deeply, perhaps for this reason. It was very usual, when a young officer was ordered into the trenches, for him to ride down to Spring Hill to dine, or obtain something more than his ordinary fare to brighten his weary hours in those fearful ditches. They seldom failed on these occasions to shake me by the hand at parting, and sometimes would say, 'You see, Mrs Seacole, I can't say good-bye to the dear ones at home, so I'll bid you good-bye for them. Perhaps you'll see them some day, and if the Russians should knock me over, mother, just tell them I thought of them all – will you?' And although all this might be said in a light-hearted manner, it was rather solemn. I felt it to be so, for I never failed (although who was I, that I should preach?) to say something about God's providence and relying upon it; and they were very good. No army of parsons could be much better than my sons. They would listen very gravely, and shake me by the hand again, while I felt that there was nothing in the world I would not do for them. Then very often the men would say, 'I'm going in with my master to-night, Mrs Seacole; come and look after him, if he's hit;' and so often as this happened I would pass the night restlessly, awaiting with anxiety the

morning, and yet dreading to hear the news it held in store
for me. I used to think it was like having a large family of
children ill with fever, and dreading to hear which one had
passed away in the night.

And as often as the bad news came, I thought it my duty
to ride up to the hut of the sufferer and do my woman's
work. But I felt it deeply. How could it be otherwise? There
was one poor boy in the Artillery, with blue eyes and light
golden hair, whom I nursed through a long and weary
sickness, borne with all a man's spirit, and whom I grew to
love like a fond old-fashioned mother. I thought if ever
angels watched over any life, they would shelter his; but
one day, but a short time after he had left his sick-bed, he
was struck down on his battery, working like a young hero.
It was a long time before I could banish from my mind the
thought of him as I saw him last, the yellow hair, stiff and
stained with his life-blood, and the blue eyes closed in the
sleep of death. Of course, I saw him buried, as I did poor
HV, my old Jamaica friend, whose kind face was so familiar
to me of old. Another good friend I mourned bitterly –
Captain B, of the Coldstreams – a great cricketer. He had
been with me on the previous evening, had seemed dull, but
had supped at my store, and on the following morning a
brother officer told me he was shot dead while setting his
picket,* which made me ill and unfit for work for the whole
day. Mind you, a day was a long time to give to sorrow in
the Crimea.

I could give many other similar instances, but why
should I sadden myself or my readers? Others have
described the horrors of those fatal trenches; but their real
history has never been written, and perhaps it is as well
that so harrowing a tale should be left in oblivion. Such
anecdotes as the following were very current in the Camp,
but I have no means of answering for its truth. Two
sergeants met in the trenches, who had been schoolmates
in their youth; years had passed since they set out for the
battle of life by different roads, and now they met again

* picket: posting groups of sentries for the night

under the fire of a common enemy. With one impulse they started forward to exchange the hearty hand-shake and the mutual greetings, and while their hands were still clasped, a chance shot killed both.

Long Walk to Freedom:
The Autobiography of Nelson Mandela

Nelson Mandela

Nelson Mandela's autobiography was published in 1994, four years after his release from what was to have been a life sentence. His remarkable life story begins in the tiny village of Qunu, where he was born the son of a Thembu chief and where villagers slept on mats in round huts woven from grass.

Chance took him away from his beloved village to be educated and to discover the injustices of apartheid in South Africa. In the course of his struggle to free black Africans from these injustices, he was imprisoned on Robben Island for thirty years. The outside world tried to persuade his country to release him and reject apartheid, and in support of his cause, many public places in England were named after him. He fought for the abolition of apartheid until it was finally vanquished in 1994.

In May 1994, Mandela was democratically elected president of South Africa by his country's people, no matter what colour their skin was. His deputy was Mr de Klerk, one-time leader of the 'white' government. The two men, former enemies, shook hands and Mandela told De Klerk: 'We are going to face the problems of this country together.'

The country does indeed face great difficulties and Mandela acknowledges this in the second of these two extracts from his autobiography, begun in jail and completed when he was seventy-six.

The first extract, taken from the section called 'Robben Island: The dark years', shows Mandela acting as spokesperson and leader for the jailed men.

W e were awakened at 5.30 each morning by the night warder, who clanged a brass bell at the head of our corridor and yelled, *'Word wakker! Staan op!'* ('Wake up! Get up!') I have always been an early riser and this hour was not a burden to me. Although we were roused at 5.30, we were not let out of our cells until 6.45, by which time we were meant to have cleaned our cells and rolled up our mats and blankets. We had no running water in our cells and instead of toilets had iron sanitary buckets known as 'ballies'. The ballies had a diameter of ten inches with a concave porcelain lid on the top that could contain water. The water in this lid was meant to be used for shaving and to clean our hands and faces.

At 6.45, when we were let out of our cells, the first thing we did was to empty our ballies. The ballies had to be thoroughly cleansed in the sinks at the end of the corridor or they created a stench. The only pleasant thing about cleaning one's ballie was that this was the one moment in those early days when we could have a whispered word with our colleagues. The warders did not like to linger when we cleaned them, so it was a chance to talk softly.

During those first few months, breakfast was delivered to us in our cells by prisoners from the general section. Breakfast consisted of mealie pap porridge, cereal made from maize or corn, which the general prisoners would slop in a bowl and then spin through the bars of our cells. It was a clever trick and required a deft hand so as not to spill any of the porridge.

After a few months, breakfast was delivered to us in the courtyard in old metal drums. We would help ourselves to pap using simple metal bowls. We each received a mug of what was described as coffee, but which was in fact ground-up maize, baked until it was black, and then brewed with hot water. Later, when we were able to go into the courtyard to serve ourselves, I would go out there and jog around the perimeter until breakfast arrived.

Like everything else in prison, diet is discriminatory. In general, Coloureds and Indians received a slightly better diet than Africans, but it was not much of a distinction. The authorities liked to say that we received a balanced diet; it was indeed balanced – between the unpalatable and the inedible. Food was the source of many of our protests, but in those early days, the warders would say, 'Ag, you kaffirs are eating better in prison than you ever ate at home!'

In the midst of breakfast, the guards would yell, *'Val in! Val in!'* ('Fall in! Fall in!'), and we would stand outside our cells for inspection. Each prisoner was required to have the three buttons of his khaki jacket properly buttoned. We were required to doff our hats as the warder walked by. If our buttons were undone, our hats unremoved, or our cells untidy, we were charged with a violation of the prison code and punished with either solitary confinement or the loss of meals.

After inspection we would work in the courtyard hammering stones until noon. There were no breaks; if we slowed down, the warders would yell at us to speed up. At noon, the bell would clang for lunch and another metal drum of food would be wheeled into the courtyard. For Africans, lunch consisted of boiled mealies, that is, coarse kernels of corn. The Indians and Coloured prisoners received samp, or mealie rice, which consisted of ground mealies in a soup-like mixture. The samp was sometimes served with vegetables, whereas our mealies were served straight.

For lunch we often received *phuzamandla*, which means 'drink of strength', a powder made from mealies and a bit of yeast. It is meant to be stirred into water or milk, and when it is thick it can be tasty, but the prison authorities gave us so little of the powder that it barely coloured the water. I would usually try to save my powder for several days until I had enough to make a proper drink, but if the authorities discovered that you were hoarding food, the powder was confiscated and you were punished.

After lunch we worked until 4, when the guards blew shrill whistles and we once again lined up to be counted and inspected. We were then permitted half an hour to clean up. The bathroom at the end of our corridor had two seawater showers, a saltwater tap and three large galvanized metal buckets, which were used as bathtubs. There was no hot water. We would stand or squat in these buckets, soaping ourselves with the brackish water, rinsing off the dust from the day. To wash yourself with cold water when it is cold outside is not pleasant, but we made the best of it. We would sometimes sing while washing, which made the water seem less icy. In those early days, this was one of the only times when we could converse.

Precisely at 4.30 there would be a loud knock on the wooden door at the end of our corridor, which meant that supper had been delivered. Common-law prisoners used to dish out the food to us and we would return to our cells to eat it. We again received mealie pap porridge, sometimes with the odd carrot or piece of cabbage or beetroot thrown in – but one usually had to search for it. If we did get a vegetable, we would usually have the same one for weeks on end, until the carrots or cabbages were old and mouldy and we were thoroughly sick of them. Every other day we received a small piece of meat with our porridge. The meat was usually mostly gristle.

For supper, Coloured and Indian prisoners received a quarter loaf of bread (known as a *katkop*, that is, a cat's head, after the shape of the bread) and a slab of margarine. Africans, it was presumed, did not care for bread as it was a 'European' type of food.

Typically, we received even less than the scanty amounts stipulated in the regulations. This was because the kitchen was rife with smuggling. The cooks – all of whom were common-law prisoners – kept the best food for themselves or their friends. Often they would lay aside the tastiest morsels for the warders in exchange for favours or preferential treatment.

At 8pm the night warder would lock himself in the corridor with us, passing the key through a small hole in the door to another warder outside. The warder would then walk up and down the corridor, ordering us to go to sleep. No cry of 'lights out' was ever given on Robben Island because the single mesh-covered bulb in our cell burned day and night. Later, those studying for higher degrees were permitted to read until 10 or 11pm.

The acoustics along the corridor were quite good, and we would try to chat a bit to each other before going to sleep. But if we could hear a whisper quite clearly, so could the warder, who would yell, '*Stilte in die gang!*' ('Quiet in the passage!') The warder would walk up and down a few times to make sure we were not reading or writing. After a few months, we would sprinkle a handful of sand along the corridor so that we could hear the warder's footsteps and have time to stop talking or hide any contraband. Only when we were quiet did he take a seat in the small office at the end of the passage where he dozed until morning.

Here Mandela writes as President of South Africa.

On the day of the inauguration, I was overwhelmed with a sense of history. In the first decade of the twentieth century, a few years after the bitter Anglo-Boer war and before my own birth, the white-skinned peoples of South Africa patched up their differences and erected a system of racial domination against the dark-skinned peoples of their own land. The structure they created formed the basis of one of the harshest, most inhumane, societies the world has ever known. Now, in the last decade of the twentieth century, and my own eighth decade as a man, that system had been overturned forever and replaced by one that recognized the rights and freedoms of all peoples regardless of the colour of their skin.

That day had come about through the unimaginable sacrifices of thousands of my people, people whose suffering and courage can never be counted or repaid. I felt that day, as I have on so many other days, that I was simply the sum of all those African patriots who had gone before me. That long and noble line ended and now began again with me. I was pained that I was not able to thank them and that they were not able to see what their sacrifices had wrought.

The policy of apartheid created a deep and lasting wound in my country and my people. All of us will spend many years, if not generations, recovering from that profound hurt. But the decades of oppression and brutality had another, unintended, effect, and that was that it produced the Oliver Tambos, the Walter Sisulus, the Chief Luthulis, the Yusuf Dadoos, the Bram Fischers, the Robert Sobukwes of our time – men of such extraordinary courage, wisdom and generosity that their like may never be known again. Perhaps it requires such depths of oppression to create such heights of character. My country is rich in the minerals and gems that lie beneath its soil, but I have always known that its greatest wealth is its people, finer and truer than the purest diamonds.

It is from these comrades in the struggle that I learned the meaning of courage. Time and again, I have seen men and women risk and give their lives for an idea. I have seen men stand up to attacks and torture without breaking, showing a strength and resilience that defies the imagination. I learned that courage was not the absence of fear, but the triumph over it. I felt fear myself more times than I can remember, but I hid it behind a mask of boldness. The brave man is not he who does not feel afraid, but he who conquers that fear.

I never lost hope that this great transformation would occur. Not only because of the great heroes I have already cited, but because of the courage of the ordinary men and women of my country. I always knew that deep down in every human heart, there was mercy and generosity. No one is born hating another person because of the colour of his skin, or his background, or his religion. People must learn to hate, and if they can learn to hate, they can be taught to love, for love comes more naturally to the human heart than its opposite. Even in the grimmest times in prison, when my comrades and I were pushed to our limits, I would see a glimmer of humanity in one of the guards, perhaps just for a second, but it was enough to reassure me and keep me going. Man's goodness is a flame that can be hidden but never extinguished.

We took up the struggle with our eyes wide open, under no illusion that the path would be an easy one. As a young man, when I joined the African National Congress, I saw the price my comrades paid for their beliefs, and it was high. For myself, I have never regretted my commitment to the struggle, and I was always prepared to face the hardships that affected me personally. But my family paid a terrible price, perhaps too dear a price, for my commitment.

In life, every man has twin obligations – obligations to his family, to his parents, to his wife and children; and he has an obligation to his people, his community, his country. In a civil and humane society, each man is able to fulfil those obligations according to his own inclinations and abilities. But in a country like South Africa, it was almost impossible for a man of my birth and colour to fulfil both of those obligations. In South Africa, a man of colour who attempted to live as a human being was punished and isolated. In South Africa, a man who tried to fulfil his duty to his people was inevitably ripped from his family and his home and was forced to live a life apart, a twilight existence of secrecy and rebellion. I did not in the beginning choose to place my people above my family, but in attempting to serve my people, I found that I was prevented from fulfilling my obligations as a son, a brother, a father and a husband.

In that way, my commitment to my people, to the millions of South Africans I would never know or meet, was at the expense of the people I knew best and loved most. It was as simple and yet as incomprehensible as the moment a small child asks her father, 'Why can you not be with us?' And the father must utter the terrible words: 'There are other children like you, a great many of them ...' and then one's voice trails off.

I was not born with a hunger to be free. I was born free – free in every way that I could know. Free to run in the fields near my mother's hut, free to swim in the clear stream that ran through my village, free to roast mealies under the stars and ride the broad backs of slow-moving bulls. As long as I obeyed my father and abided by the customs of my tribe, I was not troubled by the laws of man or God.

It was only when I began to learn that my boyhood freedom was an illusion, when I discovered as a young man that my freedom had already been taken from me, that I began to hunger for it. At first, as a student, I wanted freedom only for myself, the transitory freedoms of being able to stay out at night, read what I pleased and go where I chose. Later, as a young man in Johannesburg, I yearned for the basic and honourable freedoms of achieving my potential, of earning my keep, of marrying and having a family – the freedom not to be obstructed in a lawful life.

But then I slowly saw that not only was I not free, but my brothers and sisters were not free. I saw that it was not just my freedom that was curtailed, but the freedom of everyone who looked like I did. That is when I joined the African National Congress, and that is when the hunger for my own freedom became the greater hunger for the freedom of my people. It was this desire for the freedom of my people to live their lives with dignity and self-respect that animated my life, that transformed a frightened young man into a bold one, that drove a law-abiding attorney to become a criminal, that turned a family-loving husband into a man without a home, that forced a life-loving man to live like a monk. I am no more virtuous or self-sacrificing than the next man, but I found that I could not even enjoy the poor and limited freedoms I was allowed when I knew my people were not free. Freedom is indivisible; the chains on any one of my people were the chains on all of them, the chains on all of my people were the chains on me.

It was during those long and lonely years that my hunger for the freedom of my own people became a hunger for the freedom of all people, white and black. I knew as well as I knew anything that the oppressor must be liberated just as surely as the oppressed. A man who takes away another man's freedom is a prisoner of hatred, he is locked behind the bars of prejudice and narrow-mindedness. I am not truly free if I am taking away someone else's freedom, just as surely as I am not free when my freedom is taken from me. The oppressed and the oppressor alike are robbed of their humanity.

When I walked out of prison, that was my mission, to liberate the oppressed and the oppressor both. Some say that has now been achieved. But I know that that is not the case. The truth is that we are not yet free; we have merely achieved the freedom to be free, the right not to be oppressed. We have not taken the final step of our journey, but the first step on a longer and even more difficult road. For to be free is not merely to cast off one's chains, but to live in a way that respects and enhances the freedom of others. The true test of our devotion to freedom is just beginning.

I have walked that long road to freedom. I have tried not to falter; I have made missteps along the way. But I have discovered the secret that after climbing a great hill, one only finds that there are many more hills to climb. I have taken a moment here to rest, to steal a view of the glorious vista that surrounds me, to look back on the distance I have come. But I can rest only for a moment, for with freedom come responsibilities, and I dare not linger, for my long walk is not yet ended.

Letters

As with diaries and journals, the issue of privacy can sometimes be a concern with letters. In those following, *Mark Twain's Letters from Hawaii* are of a public kind, written to entertain newspaper readers back home in America, allowing them to see something of South Sea islands which still intrigue many of us today. He was writing letters to make a living, which is not true of other writers in this section.

Letters written to family and loved ones are often very personal. Edward Bawden was famous for his drawings and watercolours of World War II (on display in the Imperial War Museum) and sometimes wrote to the War Artists' Commission to try to speed up payments to his wife Charlotte and their children. His vivid letters to Charlotte are not about business but about his hope that he will soon return to the family.

Public and private letters show us the different roles all of us play in life. Most in this section are sent home from faraway places to give an impression of life and conditions in other countries. Others are intensely personal, like *Sarah's Letters*, which chronicle an inner journey, tracing the progress of the writer as she travels through a difficult phase in her life.

Sarah's Letters: A Case of Shyness

Bernard T. Harrison

When she was in Year 11 Sarah began writing letters to her English teacher, Dr Harrison, just before Christmas and she continued to do so for two years. It began almost as a rebellion against doing the homework that had been set. Some students reject authority at school and show this in anti-social behaviour. Sarah reacted differently, becoming more and more withdrawn from her peers, communicating in letters and at great length with a trusted adult.

Some of her anguish may have been a result of moving home, and then school too, in a short space of time. Certainly, she experienced difficulties making friends, and her teachers generally found her quiet and shy. At her grammar school, she knew how much she wanted to become a teacher, but she became disheartened by her slow progress. She asked to move school, but in doing so, she lost friends and became more isolated. Sarah gladly agreed that her letters should be used by Dr Harrison for the booklet from which the extracts were taken.

Here, in an extract from the first and longest letter, she tells her teacher something about her background.

When I started the grammar school we had just moved to the house we live in now. As we had moved from our neighbours and friends I suppose I felt even more lonely. I did feel lonely: more than I had ever felt before. We used to live on a council estate, we had lived there almost eleven years. All the children there had grown up together and so we all played together. Our house was only two bedroomed and was semi-detached. It was untidy but warm. Us five children slept in the largest bedroom. It was terrible really, we had just enough room to walk between the beds, but we usually jumped on the beds to get across the room. Often when we were in bed we would hear the girl next door chasing her younger brother up the stairs and then the slam of a door. The boy was one and a half years older than me and his sister was three years older than him. They and their parents are some of the kindest and most good people I have ever known. They have faults, haven't we all? Every one of them was in the habit of exaggerating and being slightly big-headed but they were not cruel and hard. They never meant any harm by it. I suppose I liked them having so much confidence in themselves because I lacked this and they seemed to give me more confidence. They would do anything for us and I think my mum and dad would do anything for them. I do not think you would meet such good friends anywhere else in the world. My mum and dad would agree with that. My dad and sister were not so close to our neighbours as my mum and me. They preferred their own company. If they were happy like that I am glad but one thing my mum and I have in common is the need for this warmth. My mum misses our neighbours but she has made friends with women who are not snobbish like the women in our road. Truthfully I don't think I want anybody to take the place of my old neighbours. I suppose I won't make the effort but I find it hard to go out so I do not meet people. It is not people of my own age who I lack a warmth from. I have got friends like Sandra and Gill. It is older people. People my mum's age. I do not know why I enjoy this sort of company. I just feel at ease and relaxed. Our neighbours here dislike children and are forever telling my brothers to be quiet when they are playing in the garden. During the summer holidays I was sitting in the garden while my brothers were playing. They were making a noise but it was not very loud. The lady next door was watching them with absolute disgust but as soon as my mum came out into the garden she was all smiles. Why do people want to dislike children? Children mess up the house and garden. Our house is the untidiest house in our part of the road, but what does it matter? My old neighbours loved children. When I was young I used to help my aunt Nell (we called her that) do her housework. Out of the children in my family I was the one who lived in their warmth most. In summer I would come home from school and find my mum sitting in the garden talking to my aunt Nell as they drank their tea. I loved sitting with them and listening to them talking. They might be standing on the doorstep talking to a couple of other women from the estate. I suppose people would say this was wasting time but it wasn't, not to me. It was lovely coming home from school seeing my mum and aunt talking and watching my little brothers playing on the grass in front of the house. They were often laughing and joking. As I turned the corner into my road I could see my mum and aunt. I used to run as fast as I could to get home and see my brothers and mum and dad. It was safer than where we live now. Very few cars came there because the road curved into a circle so you ended up where you had started. There were two greens which we played on and we also had a back garden and a front garden. The front gardens were all open but where we live now people have their gardens boxed in. The top part of our garden was a dump but lovely. We had a little house and a slide which my dad had built for us but they were falling to bits because of age and the rough wear they had suffered. My brothers had dug an enormous hole in the middle of the garden but they had hours of fun digging so my dad decided not to stop them. I think this was very kind of him because I know he would like a really beautiful garden and yet he gave his own pleasure up for my little brothers. Not a lot of parents are so unselfish as my mum and dad.

In the evening my brother Stephen, David and Jackie (the boy and girl from next door) my best friend, myself and a few other children used to go to the heath which joined onto the estate and played rounders or some other game. The air would become quite cool towards eight o'clock but I did not feel cold, I felt alive. Quite often we played in front of our houses and sometimes on the shed roofs which joined the back gardens. If it was hot we sometimes had picnics of our own on the roof or over the heath. We stayed out playing until it was quite dark because we felt safe, we had plenty of playing space and there were no main roads. My mum and dad did not work so hard as they do now and they joined in the fun with us. Sometimes on Sunday afternoons my dad used to take us over to the part of the heath which was on the other side of the main road. My dad used to chase us among the trees and when he caught us he tickled us. All my friends used to come and really he was like a dad to them as well. They all liked him a lot because he joined in the games with us and we felt he wanted to. We ran amongst the trees and ferns, stained our clothes and getting altogether filthy; but who cared. I loved the trees as they wavered in the wind and the ferns turning golden brown; I loved my dad. My dad did so many things for us I could never write them.

I want my youngest brothers to have this love as well. Ian is eight and Matthew is five. They need more freedom I think. My mum and dad give them freedom but they can't go out to play without an adult because of the main roads. They have toys and things like that but I do not feel children really need all the toys they have. Most boys love running about on heaths or cycling. They cannot make a lot of noise because of neighbours. My mum and dad give my brothers their attention, more than a great many parents give their children but I do not feel it is quite right. My mum and dad are older so really it is not surprising that they are not so patient as they used to be and they have to work very hard. Too hard. My dad does not get enough sleep and rest. When we were small and we asked my dad to play with us he would be pleased to but now he seems to feel while he is playing with my brothers he could be getting on with some work. I hate this because I am sure he wants to spend time with my brothers but all the time he feels there is work to do. I do not see a way out of this problem really because rates and bills have got to be paid but I feel my mum, dad and younger brother spend too much time indoors. My mum is always in the house except when she is shopping. We most probably have arguments because we are all in the house together every minute except when we are at school. Holidays are the worst times. I never go out so we all feel everybody else is in the way. I feel terrible when my brothers are fighting. One is shouting to my mum who is machining upstairs, they fight so cruelly, they seem to hate each other. They are jealous of each other and torment each other terribly; when they have been arguing all day I feel I wish I were dead. Why can't everybody be happier? I know children fight but surely not so viciously, not with so much hatred. I cannot shut the arguing out of my mind, I cannot go up to my bedroom and ignore it, it means too much to me. It should not mean a lot to me but it does. Almost everything means a lot to me whether happy or miserable. My heart aches because the one thing in the world I want is for us to be a happy family.

Some of her objections to school can be felt in this extract, written almost a year later, describing a German lesson.

I stood outside the classroom, leaning against the wall. No point in worrying now, I thought to myself, I can't conjure up homework in two minutes. I felt rather sleepy and sluggish, I could have fallen asleep had the circumstances been more attractive, still in thirty minutes time I would be able to retire to a cosy corner in the cloakroom. Peace. I realized I had been absently chewing my fingernail and I withdrew the damp finger from my mouth. Swiftly I examined each fingernail on my right hand and after a minute's consideration, I said to myself, I am glad I don't actually bite my nails, and deftly popped my finger back into my mouth. Waiting for the teacher was beginning to play on my nerves and I felt a slight agitation growing inside me. If it was I who was late, it would be, Why are you late? Explanation please. Don't let it happen again. But when it is the teacher who is late, well, that's just unfortunate. I sighed, loudly, just to make sure everybody in the immediate surroundings knew how bored I was. There was one responsive grin, so I grinned back, after all what else was there for me to do? Five of us were left standing in the silent corridor, nobody bothered to speak, but as the teacher loomed into the distance, I was aware that I was not the only person who felt disheartened. In what seemed like no time at all, I was sitting by the radiator, fumbling with a couple of books. I heard the word 'homework' mentioned but I pretended that I had not.

'Sarah! Have you got any homework for me?' she asked with some impatience.

I shook my head, my eyes averted from the direction in which the voice had come from. I had meant to be very polite, and apologize but somehow I could not cope with words, so I remained insolently silent.

'And why not?' she asked.

What a ridiculous question, I thought to myself, and just shook my head again. However, after a quick reflection I added a shrug of the shoulders and a foolish grin. I knew it was the wrong thing to do but I felt too drowsy and bored to answer such an unnecessary question. Everybody knew I was lazy.

'Tomorrow morning, then, without fail', and with that, she turned to a pile of books on the desk, while I nodded fervently, still grinning.

I sat staring out of the window while the teacher found some work for us to do. Anything she gave us was difficult, but reading out loud, now that was something worth dreading.

'Seite drei und sechzig.'

I flicked through the thick green book. Why did she always say the number of the page in German? It always took me half of the lesson just trying to find the right page.

'Martin, will you begin reading?' the teacher asked.

I perched on the edge of my chair in order to see which page his book was open at. Just as he came to the end of his passage the number of the page became apparent and I hastily turned to the page in my book.

'Carry on, Sarah,' urged the voice from the front of the classroom.

Instantly I stiffened, like a cat which was afraid, I felt hot and clammy because I was so tense, I felt useless. Everybody was waiting for me to speak and I couldn't. My throat was so dry that I knew if I tried to speak, only a croak would come out. Silence. I could have cried but that would have been of no avail. I placed my finger on the first word I was to read and I began. Slowly and toneless. Every time I pronounced a word wrong, the teacher corrected me and I had to repeat it. The more this happened the worse I felt.

I feel stranger now than I have ever felt in the last six years. Perhaps I appear a weak person to a lot of people but, I know, that I am not so weak. I admit I am rather soft and easily hurt but other people cannot sway me when I really believe something. I think I have become stronger because I feel more confident in myself and I think David and Richard have helped me a lot. People have often winked laughing at me openly, for fear of hurting me, and although at the time I was grateful, I now realise it hindered me because I always took myself and other people seriously. I could never laugh at myself because, I felt so self-conscious and inhibited that I couldn't bear any form of criticism, even if it was only a joke.

An extract from one of Sarah's letters

My fingers clutched at my cardigan, searching for something firm and my hair flopped over my eyes so that I kept losing the line I was reading from. I had read half of my passage and then, a blockage set itself in my mind. I just couldn't read any more, everything had been squeezed out of me. I sat, staring at the page. 'Can't she see I can't read anymore,' I thought to myself. 'Why doesn't she choose somebody else and leave me alone?' I bit my lip, and frowned heavily. I felt deeply resentful. Why do I have to go through this ordeal every time? I was on the verge of walking out or just crying when she said: 'Will you finish reading Paul?'

I did not sigh inside me or feel relieved. I carried on staring at the words, they were dead. I did not dare look up or show any signs of consciousness, because while I seemed dead nothing would be expected of me.

As the lesson came to an end I began to unwind. Very slowly and with uncertainty. I was the first to leave the room. Out of the clutches of tension and distress I felt like a wet rag.

Although Sarah began an A-level course, she left before taking exams, in spite of her ambition to be a teacher. However, hers is not an unhappy ending, and here she acknowledges the help she was given by two of her friends.

I feel stronger now than I have ever felt in the last six years. Perhaps I appear a weak person to a lot of people, but I know that I am not so weak. I admit I am rather soft and easily hurt but other people cannot sway me when I really believe something. I think I have become stronger because I feel more confident in myself and I think David and Richard have helped me a lot. People have often avoided laughing at me openly, for fear of hurting me, and although at the time I was grateful, I now realize it hindered me because I always took myself and other people seriously. I could never laugh at myself because I felt so self-conscious and inhibited that I could not bear any form of criticism, even if it was only a joke … David and Richard have helped me to learn how to laugh at myself because of their warmth and perseverance. When Richard first made jokes about me I felt ever so hurt and confused because I had never been really made fun of before. I used to walk into the classroom and he would call me 'Muscles', making me want to shrivel up to nothing. At the beginning I lost quite a lot of self-confidence and became more inhibited because I felt he must despise me. I really began to feel I must be weird for him to say such mad things. I do not recall feeling so hurt because of David and I think I probably felt at ease with David from the beginning. It is only very recently that I have felt able to talk to Richard, because somehow people who appear very confident in themselves make me feel uncertain of myself. I used to think I would never feel at ease with Richard but now I can talk to him and I feel grateful to him because I made no effort whatsoever to offer any friendship or warmth. It was not because I did not want to, I just could not, but Richard and David really broke through my shell and I am glad they did ...

Mark Twain's Letters from Hawaii

Mark Twain

Mark Twain, born Samuel Langhorn Clemens in 1835, is best known for his novels written for young people such as *Tom Sawyer* and *Huckleberry Finn*. He spent some of his early life as a Mississippi steamboat pilot and his pen name 'Mark Twain', meaning 'two fathoms', refers to the depth of water beneath the boat, and would be yelled out to the pilot as he steered, to help him avoid going aground in the treacherous waters. Throughout his life he travelled. For some time he tried to pay off his debts by sending letters to newspapers from the Hawaiian islands and from the Mediterranean, giving lectures on board ships while he travelled.

When he sailed to Hawaii on the *Ajax* in 1866, he was a roving correspondent for the *Sacramento Union*, an extremely influential daily and weekly newspaper which circulated on the west coast of the United States where it was read by wealthy businessmen. As soon as he arrived on the main island of Hawaii, Oahu, Twain hired a horse, named it after the island, and set off to explore and report back to his employers.

In these extracts from a long letter sent from Honolulu in March 1866, he reports on the first part of his uncomfortable sight-seeing ride. His horse is lame or exhausted and Twain clearly is a poor rider. In the letter following this one, Oahu struggles to the top of Diamond Head, an extinct volcano from which he gallops down. The village of King Kamehameha, Waikiki, which Twain describes in this letter, is today one of the most famous and expensive tourist resorts in the world.

Coming home from prison

I am probably the most sensitive man in the kingdom of Hawaii tonight – especially about sitting down in the presence of my betters. I have ridden fifteen or twenty miles on horseback since 5 pm, and to tell the honest truth, I have a delicacy about sitting down at all. I am one of the poorest horsemen in the world, and I never mount a horse without experiencing a sort of dread that I may be setting out on that last mysterious journey which all of us must take sooner or later, and I never come back in safety from a horseback trip without thinking of my latter end for two or three days afterward. This same old regular devotional sentiment began just as soon as I sat down here five minutes ago.

An excursion to Diamond Head and the King's Coconut Grove was planned today – time, 4.30 pm, – the party to consist of half a dozen gentlemen and three ladies. They all started at the appointed hour except myself. I was at the government prison, and got so interested in its examination that I did not notice how quickly the time was passing. Somebody remarked that it was twenty minutes past five o'clock, and that woke me up. It was a fortunate circumstance that Captain Phillips was there with his 'turnout,' as he calls a top buggy that Captain Cook brought here in 1778, and a horse that was here when Captain Cook came. Captain Phillips takes a just pride in his driving and in the speed of his horse, and to his passion for displaying them I owe it that we were only sixteen minutes coming from the prison to the American Hotel – a distance which has been estimated to be over half a mile. But it took some awful driving. The captain's whip came down fast, and the blows started so much dust out of the horse's hide that during the last half of the journey we rode through an impenetrable fog, and ran by a pocket compass in the hands of Captain Fish, a whaler captain of 26 years experience, who sat there through that perilous voyage as self-possessed as if he had been on the euchre-deck* of his own ship, and calmly said, 'Port your helm – port,' from time to time, and 'Hold her a little free – steady – so-o,' and 'Luff – hard down to starboard!' and never once lost his presence of mind or betrayed the least anxiety by voice or manner. When we came to anchor at last, and Captain Phillips looked at his watch and said, 'Sixteen minutes – I

* euchre-deck: the card-playing deck

told you it was in her! that's over three miles an hour!' I
could see he felt entitled to a compliment, and so I said I
had never seen lightning go like that horse. And I never
had.

The steed 'Oahu'

The landlord of the American said the party had been gone
nearly an hour, but that he could give me my choice of
several horses that could easily overtake them. I said,
never mind – I preferred a safe horse to a fast one – I would
like to have an excessively gentle horse – a horse with no
spirit whatever – a lame one, if he had such a thing. Inside
five minutes I was mounted, and perfectly satisfied with
my outfit. I had no time to label him 'This is a horse,' and
so if the public took him for a sheep, I cannot help it. I was
satisfied, and that was the main thing. I could see that he
had as many fine points as any man's horse, and I just hung
my hat on one of them, behind the saddle, and swabbed the
perspiration from my face and started. I named him after
this island, 'Oahu' (pronounced O-waw-hoo). The first gate
he came to he started in; I had neither whip nor spur, and
so I simply argued the case with him. He firmly resisted
argument, but ultimately yielded to insult and abuse. He
backed out of that gate and steered for another one on the
other side of the street. I triumphed by my former process.
Within the next 600 yards he crossed the street fourteen
times and attempted thirteen gates, and in the meantime
the tropical sun was beating down and threatening to cave
the top of my head in, and I was literally dripping with
perspiration and profanity. (I am only human and I was
sorely aggravated. I shall behave better next time.) He quit
the gate business after that and went along peaceably
enough, but absorbed in meditation. I noticed this latter
circumstance, and it soon began to fill me with the gravest
apprehension. I said to myself, this malignant brute is
planning some new outrage, some fresh devilry or other –
no horse ever thought over a subject so profoundly as this
one is doing just for nothing. The more this thing preyed
upon my mind, the more uneasy I became, until at last the
suspense became unbearable and I dismounted to see if

there was anything wild in his eye – for I had heard that the eye of this noblest of our domestic animals is very expressive. I cannot describe what a load of anxiety was lifted from my mind when I found that he was only asleep. I woke him up and started him into a faster walk, and then the inborn villainy of his nature came out again. He tried to climb over a stone wall, five or six feet high. I saw that I must apply force to this horse, and that I might as well begin first as last. I plucked a stout switch from a tamarind tree, and the moment he saw it, he gave in. He broke into a convulsive sort of a canter, which had three short steps in it and one long one, and reminded me alternately of the clattering shake of the great earthquake, and the sweeping plunging of the *Ajax* in a storm.

Out of prison, but in the stocks

And now it occurs to me that there can be no fitter occasion than the present to pronounce a fervent curse upon the man who invented the American saddle. There is no seat to speak of about it – one might as well sit in a shovel and the stirrups are nothing but an ornamental nuisance. If I were to write down here all the abuse I expended on those stirrups, it would make a large book, even without pictures. Sometimes I got one foot so far through, that the stirrup partook of the nature of an anklet; sometimes both feet were through, and I was handcuffed by the legs, and sometimes my feet got clear out and left the stirrups wildly dangling about my shins. Even when I was in proper position and carefully balanced upon the balls of my feet, there was no comfort in it, on account of my nervous dread that they were going to slip one way or the other in a moment. But the subject is too exasperating to write about.

The King's Grove, Waikiki

A mile and a half from town, I came to a grove of tall coconut trees, with clean, branchless stems reaching straight up sixty or seventy feet and topped with a spray of green foliage sheltering clusters of coconuts – not more picturesque than a forest of colossal ragged parasols, with bunches of magnified grapes under them, would be. About a dozen cottages, some frame and the others of native grass, nestled sleepily in the shade here and there. The grass cabins are of a grayish color, are shaped much like our own cottages, only with higher and steeper roofs usually, and are made of some kind of weed strongly bound together in bundles. The roofs are very thick, and so are the walls; the latter have square holes in them for windows. At a little distance these cabins have a furry appearance, as if they might be made of bear skins. They are very cool and pleasant inside. The King's flag was flying from the roof of one of the cottages, and His Majesty was probably within. He owns the whole concern thereabouts, and passes his time there frequently, on sultry days 'laying off.' The spot is called 'the King's Grove.'

* * *

The little collection of cottages under the coconut trees is a historical point. It is the village of Waikiki (usually pronounced Wy-kee-ky), once the capital of the kingdom and the abode of the great Kamehameha I. In 1801, while he lay encamped at this place with 7000 men, preparing to invade the island of Kau[a]i (he had previously captured and subdued the seven other inhabited islands of the group, one after another), a pestilence broke out in Oahu and raged with great virulence. It attacked the King's army and made great havoc in it. It is said that 300 bodies were washed out to sea in one day.

There is an opening in the coral reef at this point, and anchorage inside for a small number of vessels, though one accustomed to the great bay of San Francisco would never take this little belt of smooth water, with its border of foaming surf, to be a harbor, save for Whitehall boats or something of that kind. But harbors are scarce in these islands – open roadsteads are the rule here. The harbor of Waikiki was discovered in 1786 (seven or eight years after Captain Cook's murder) by Captains Portlock and Dixon, in the ships *King George* and *Queen Charlotte* – the first English vessels that visited the islands after that unhappy occurrence. This little bathing tub of smooth water possesses some further historical interest as being the spot where the distinguished navigator Vancouver landed when he came here in 1792.

In a conversation with a gentleman today about the scarcity of harbors among the islands (and in all the islands of the South Pacific), he said the natives of Tahiti have a theory that the reason why there are harbors wherever fresh water streams empty into the sea, and none elsewhere, is that the fresh water kills the coral insect, or so discommodes or disgusts it that it will not build its stony wall in its vicinity, and instanced what is claimed as fact, viz., that the break in the reef is always found where the fresh water passes over it, in support of this theory.

(This notable equestrian excursion will be concluded in my next, if nothing happens.)

A Letter from Jaipur

Angela Barrs

In July 1995, Angela Barrs visited northern India because she wanted to see some of the great temples and palaces of the Moghul emperors. She travelled with a group of tourists, led by Prem, who came from Kashmir, and they visited Delhi and Agra (where the Taj Mahal is) briefly before going on to the city of Jaipur. Arriving in the dark, in the monsoon season, she had no impression of the city apart from its crowds and the rain. She feels that a place is best understood by walking around in it.

Her walk the following day was also a shopping trip, for something to brighten up her very restricted choice of clothes, and for her younger brother's present. She already knew of the Hindu celebration for brothers' and sisters' day, which takes place on 10 August and has since discovered that the idea behind it of brother/sister affection extends to friendships too. In Halifax, West Yorkshire, the mayor was given a raki, a coloured thread worn around the wrist as an expression of friendship, by the Hindu and Cultural Arts Association in 1995 as a token of goodwill.

As she had not found a present to take back from India to her brother, she felt that sending him a raki with a letter explaining how she came to buy it would be a way of showing her affection.

Hotel Bissau Palace
Jaipur 302016
Thursday, 3 August 1995

Dear Little Brother,
It seemed a good idea to go out for a stroll when we got back from lunch, especially as it had stopped raining. I went off to try and buy something for you, which you have to wear on 10 August. This is the festival of brothers and sisters. People exchange 'rakis' – coloured threads worn round the wrist like friendship bracelets – as signs of

affection for each other and there are celebrations and feasts to mark it as a special day. So, even if you don't wear this at work, I hope it'll cheer you up when you get back home that day and put it on. Please show it off to friends, because you are a special brother.

Here's how I got the raki. I put on my waterproof and retraced the route we had taken the night before. The monsoon rains have burst through the town and last night we drove up what seemed to be a river. The baggage compartment in the bus got the worst of it and I was glad I'd thought to pack all my stuff in binliners inside the case. Most of it stayed dry.

First, as I came to the roundabout (last night it was a lake) I took a photo of the pigs and their piglets rooting in the rubbish which even the cows had given up on. Stepping across piles of broken bricks and general garbage, I said 'no thanks' to various traders and took a snapshot of the fish-sellers, squatting beside their wares with clouds of flies around them. I wandered through the vegetable and fruit market. This was almost like an outdoor market at home but what glorious vegetables! I said 'hello' to several women stall-holders, which caused us all to giggle and then none of us could stop laughing because we couldn't say any more to each other. 'Hello' produced a wonderful effect on us all. Past the Brahmin cows and calves I went, they and I ambling across bus lanes and then in through one of the old town gateways – rose-red and only just wide enough for one careful bus. Under the high archway people continued to trade, leaning against the huge iron-studded doors. Beneath the smaller arches at either side more business was going on. Ahead through the gates the busy traffic, even the overladen trucks, has to do a sharp left, right, left around two tiny square temples in the middle of the road. To honour the god or goddess in these temples, you place an offering inside, frequently a garland of marigolds, the Hindu special colour, or other auspicious flowers. Prem has booked us a table for tonight in what was once the maharajah's palace and he said that they preferred formal-ish clothes there, but I haven't got anything smart. I'll put on the best I've got and dress it up with a garland or two. I also wanted to take photos of the flower-sellers because the orange, white and scarlet heaps of blossoms are magnificent.

So, I asked the first trader what price he wanted for a garland of jasmine. The flowers are white and not so vivid as marigolds but the perfume is heady. He said 'two rupees' so I thought I'd wait and buy some on the way back.

I found a shop which I thought might sell rakis and asked them about their display. The first rakis I was shown were enormous things with appliques and sequins and you'd have needed wrestlers' arms to show them off. Then I was shown ones with tinsel – tacky perhaps but very popular. I chose this little leaf-shaped one on a red cord and after haggling, agreed a price but had to wait for change. Whilst I waited, a street photographer snapped me, but I didn't want his photo – my picture will bring plenty of business to the shop. 'Even English women buy my rakis!' he will say to his friends. The change was short and after putting that right, I decided on two jasmine garlands as I've no glamorous jewellery to wear. (I spent an interesting half-hour with Lynne earlier being an onlooker while she bought a beautiful gold-set emerald ring flanked with mini-diamonds – £186. A snip in English terms and a fortune to the average Indian.) On the way back, the flower-seller looked glum in the drizzle but seemed amazed that I'd come back for the jasmine.

Avoiding the tricycle-rickshaws, and seeing no camel-carts about, I waded through rivulets and missed the hotel entrance. However, a peacock among the pigeons on the telegraph wire seemed a good photo opportunity. A young man came up and asked was I staying at the Hotel Bissau Palace because if I was I'd missed my way. I said yes but I wasn't lost, thank you, but taking a photo. He offered to show me a much better place for peacocks – but I declined. (An enterprising try for a tip.)

In the hotel garden, I stood in a deep puddle to wash the muck off my trainers. I shan't bring *them* home, but left in the hotel, they will bring a handsome profit when resold by staff; nothing, but nothing, is ever thrown away – what a contrast with the way we live at home.

A cup of black tea on the terrace among the flies and rotting rattan furniture and then I'll get ready for a night on the town.

This is the nicest and strangest hotel we've stayed in yet. It's a haveli – a rich merchant's ex-pad and I'm sharing a room in the stable block. Everything functions. Behind my bed to the right is an enormous extractor fan. You can hardly hear the other person speak when it's on so we're making do with the ceiling fan. It makes a lovely breeze for drying damp clothes washed last night. I took a picture of the two beds. Between them there is almost no space at all. You vault into them onto very solid mattresses that smell of many monsoons. The head and footboards are very like the hallstands in old-fashioned houses. There are mirrors and pictures set in amongst the wooden twirls. In the morning you can kneel at the foot of the bed to see if you've brushed your hair neatly enough.

The maharajah of Jaipur used to come out to banquets here and when we arrived last night, I read the menu for one such banquet he ate in 1932, all fifteen courses, eight wines and the complete band programme. The place is full of photos of him and his family.

Wear your raki for me.

Love from Angela

Edward Bawden's Letters Home
1940–45

Edward Bawden

In 1939, at the age of 36, Edward Bawden, a married man with two young children, went off to France in order to draw and paint World War II in action. He was employed by the War Artists' Advisory Committee and from then until the end of the war he spent very little time with his family. Before the war, he had worked successfully illustrating cookery books, designing posters on the London Underground and drawing for advertisements. In addition to recording the military events in drawings and paintings, he kept in touch with his family by writing to his wife Charlotte, also a painter, to his father, and to his employers on the committee.

His travels took him through Europe, Middle Eastern cities such as Damascus and Baghdad, and finally back to Europe. On a journey to visit the Marsh Arabs in Iraq, the ship he was travelling on, the *Laconia*, was torpedoed and he was rescued after spending four nights on a life raft, surrounded by sharks. He and other British officers were rescued by the French ship *Gloire* but the ship was collaborating with the German army and the rescued soldiers were held as prisoners of war. Officially categorized as a war correspondent, he was later given the honorary title of 'Captain'.

Bawden drew and painted in extreme conditions, in the desert for example, sweating into the ink he used whilst actually drawing. His letters to his wife show a man longing to be home. The two here were written near the end of the war. After writing the letter from Rome, he had to wait until August before he was reunited with his family.

23 March, 1945

Charlotte my dear, ... The jeep was at the Hotel by nine. The maps I had collected didn't mean a great deal, – from the coloured contour lines I couldn't visualize the

country. Unlike Italy the shape of Greece is not easy to fix
in the mind, its edges are blurred by constellations of
jigsaw puzzle islands and not all the names of places trip
off the tongue on first sight of the printed word; and
distances, unless one has roamed across a country have an
unreality on the map, – often it is not miles that comprise
a reckoning but the number of hours taken. I noticed that
I should be passing through Thebes and skirting the slopes
of Parnassus.

Yesterday we did 240 miles. I didn't sleep well at night
because of being arse-sore, and today was wretchedly
uncomfortable doing 160 sitting on the same hard seat. At
half past five we reached the camp in the foothills. On the
way a short stop at another headquarters had to be made;
on advice I narrowed the field of choice to a certain locality,
– again a signal was sent in advance. The camp occupied
the buildings and baths of a small spa. The Padre and I
were both late for the tea hour and we became acquainted
by sharing a specially brewed pot. He was a small,
dark-browed Welshman and a fervent talker, a chirpy
oracle on any serious topic, and for my benefit he reviewed
the Parthenon, Michelangelo, Raphael and suchlike
matters with an enthusiasm which made me feel shy of
adding coals to his own blaze: he had read recently a
Philosophy of Art, a Philosophy of Nudism and Beverley
Nichols' book on India – the blaze, and certainly it gave out
a great deal of warmth, resembled an electric heater that
has coloured glass flames in artificial logs. Am I doing the
Padre an injustice? His sincerity was alright but his ideas,
like an electric current, derived from other sources and
weren't due to spontaneous combustion. A glib
interpretation of things which cannot be rightly expressed
in words is boring. On the other hand I made use of his
friendliness, and of his batman. The camp had a fine site
on the slope of a hill, among other steep hills, and there was
a skyline of snowy mountain peaks; down below, a river ran
in meandering channels through a wide, stony bed in the
valley. In Greece good scenery is a commonplace. The
incomparable luxury was sulphur springs – clouds of steam
rose from some in the distance – but on this hillside the

warm water was piped into a converted swimming pool. In summer the temperature increased so I was told. Hot baths had been scarce enough in Italy: I didn't need to bear in mind the few satisfactory washings I had had, – I rushed off for a towel and then to the pool. The Padre had beat me to it! a clerical head was sticking out of the water.

25 March, 1945

I went into a nearby town to see the Independence Day procession: from an upstairs window in the main square I had an excellent view, sitting outside on the window-sill with my feet on the tiles. The procession was of the sort to be expected from the resources of a small country town. The local band in nondescript khaki uniforms led off the proceedings by blowing and banging in great style. There was a cluster of shimmering blue and white flags followed by the priests in long, stiff, golden vestments. The order of the different groups that formed up and marched into place as the procession uncoiled eludes my memory, – there was the President of the town and his Councillors respectably dressed in black, parties of young men and girls in the national dress of each province...

* * *

The camp was pitched midway between the town to which I went on Independence Day, and a large village in the mountains that had been destroyed by German troops as a reprisal. Scores of other lesser villages in the mountains had been treated in the same way; I passed through several which had been blown up and burnt out, one hamlet completely in ruins I noticed in particular because the people there had erected a poor little arch of poles over the road and tied green leafy boughs on to it in honour of the Anniversary (the overthrow of the Turks in 1821) and, at the top of the arch they had crossed the Greek flag with the Union Jack over a piece of cloth stretched taut on which was painted the words 'Welcome my friend'. It was a very touching tribute.

* * *

A young Major who commanded the Company stationed in the village received me. We strolled up to see the Mayor, or President as he was called, as I had a parcel of news-sheets in Greek to deliver. He was a shrewd, affable, nervous, excitable man. Over glasses of ouzo, a fiery clear spirit that becomes milky by the addition of water, the talk turned on yesterday's celebrations of Greek Independence. There had been a flutter. As the Mayor was in the act of laying a wreath at the foot of the monument in the main square a small band of Communists chose that moment for a demonstration; the Mayor hesitated, but the young Major who had lined up a Guard of Honour gave the order, – 'Present Arms'. The communists seeing rifles being brought into position with clicks of precision feared that they were going to be fired upon and fled. Thereupon the Mayor deposited the wreath and the proceedings went off OK. The monument in the main square consisted of the bust of a General on a pedestal, and it commemorated his death with a handful of men against overwhelming Turkish odds in a local Thermopilae. One evening sitting in the square with the Mayor and the Major drinking ouzo I asked about this General. In rapid, difficult English to catch by ear, the Mayor explained how the camp had been overrun by Turks at night and the General had died fighting in his tent: on one point he was emphatic, 'He just crazy man, – all General crazy' – alas, how often is this the epithet bestowed by posterity on heroes!

On another day communists held a meeting in a house. As political meetings of this character are at present forbidden by law the Mayor had those who were attending it arrested. Then the difficulty arose what should be done with them, – to send the party under police escort to the nearest town would require transport, and that wasn't forthcoming. When appealed to for help the Major rightly washed his hands of the business: it was a matter for the Greeks to settle amongst themselves, he said. What was the alternative? – only to set them free. For their part the communists were highly incensed – why had they been arrested at the instigation of the British – it was only a wedding breakfast, they said!

* * *

I shared a tent with the Major: we were all under canvas. It wasn't too bad. About seven it became too chilly for sitting outdoors in the square, and wishing goodnight to the Mayor we walked 'home' tapping the roadway with our shepherd's crooks; but before we slid down the 150 feet bank to the encampment in the almond orchard we called in at the cookhouse for a mug of tea, to stand for a minute or two drinking it by the hot petrol blaze roaring under the cooker.

* * *

The young Major was a first rate chap. He had a happy knack of being able always to strike the right sort of balance, which gives behaviour the appearance of easy naturalness: he was never on or off his dignity, his friendliness did not cloak familiarity, he was good-humoured on all occasions and thoughtful in seeing to the comfort of his men, never complained or showed signs of worry but in every way he was willing to be helpful. He was also a first-rate officer and had been badly wounded in Italy: the best testimonial is the unsolicited, – his batman could have said nothing better than 'The Major was always with his men.' With him was another officer – they were peacetime friends – whom I liked nearly as well. Both of them were a great success with the local Greek authorities: it seemed to me a pity that such excellent men would go back to their peacetime jobs, respectively dealing with insurance claims and workmen's compensations, when, above all, they belonged to the type who could represent their country abroad – as I should have thought – more honourably than the public school nitwits who get these Government posts by having an uncle in the Foreign Office.

This letter has reached a tiresome length – for you as a reader! Well, I'm sorry if it seems to dribble on – how do you like this snap of myself taken by a young woman in Athens?

With love to you, dearest,
Edward

Rome
2 May, 1945

Charlotte my dear, … If I come home at the end of June I shall be living at Cheltenham until we can move to Brick House. That won't be possible for some time and I should say it would not be advisable to do so until it is possible to get repairs done, – perhaps it might mean two years more in Cheltenham. My plan is to make some money quickly – (I ought to get a nice windfall when allowances are paid and I'll send a claim off in the next few days) – secondly I would like to give you a good long break if our finances will permit, anyway the holiday you deserve to have after those long war years of drudgery. If only we could get to Greece I believe you would find the change immensely refreshing, – and we both could paint! That would be the ideal solution – with a tent and a bakers' van one could get about and live anywhere, among magnificent scenery and under blue skies. But then there's the question of the children's education – depressing I feel because it's a long and senseless routine, deadening in its effect on most children. Parental influence is also bad for children if they have to suffer too much of Dad and Mum's pet prejudices. I wish children would go off and live together in caves until they're grown up and fit to return to the company of other grown ups: I would send them off willingly with a bow and some arrows, and a copy of Lord Chesterfield's Letters. Also getting children civilized is an expensive business – just at the age when they ought to be tearing up hills and exploring a tough countryside they must sit at desks doing geography from books! Dear, dear! I'm not being helpful in the least – but I do hate the system.

News has just come of the surrender of the Italian and German armies in Italy. I don't know how this will affect me, but I presume, if Germany doesn't capitulate in the next few days that I shall go into enemy territory, – I feel dazed by the rapidity of recent events, but increasingly hopeful of being back home by the end of June.

My dearest, I do look forward to seeing you again.

With love,
Edward

Travel

Men and women have always travelled and the idea of literally travelling round the world has been with us for centuries. The great Elizabethan explorers were motivated to sail round the world to find a quicker route from Europe to India, the land of valuable spices and gemstones. Fictional travellers have made that journey, such as the hero of Jules Verne's novel *Around the World in Eighty Days* and people like Richard Branson (in a hot-air balloon) and Michael Palin have tried and sometimes succeeded. Two real people have completed a circumnavigation according to the rules of the *Guinness Book of Records*. Ffyona Campbell took up that challenge and you can read part of her account of her walk across Africa, and across the world, in the first extract in this section.

You can see in this section the difference in the technology of travel now and in earlier times. Amelia Edwards, a Victorian traveller, went up the Nile on a wooden boat, hauled up the rapids by sheer human effort. By contrast Ffyona Campbell, although she walked on foot all the way through Africa, had a back-up team with a Land Rover, packed with today's essentials, such as water purifiers, sunscreen and antibiotics. Even Christina Dodwell had a 'state-of-the-art' inflatable boat, but she almost lost it – as her predecessor almost lost a boat made of animal skins. Travellers are sometimes criticized for escaping from the reality of everyday life. The tourist and holidaymaker know they will return home after a fortnight or so. Perhaps they envy travellers their longer time to explore other places. We can choose to shut ourselves into our own worlds, widen our horizons by travelling, or if that can't be managed, by reading travel writing. As our world shrinks, with the new technologies allowing us to access information on the Internet and e-mail in no time at all, we may be in danger of experiencing too much at second-hand. All the writers in this section wanted to see for themselves.

On Foot through Africa

Ffyona Campbell

Fyona Campbell's walk from the bottom to the top of Africa took two years to prepare. It would have been a copy of the old explorers' route, but the dangers of war in some African countries prevented this more direct trip north. Although she walked the whole way herself (approximately 16,000 kilometres), she had a small back-up team of two drivers and a Land Rover. The drivers changed at various stages, but Ffyona went on with new teams. She divided her walking day into quarters and the Land Rover drove ahead to prepare drinks and meal-stops. Several sponsors helped finance her walk and the charity Survival International benefited from money she raised. Aged 24, she set off from Cape Town, South Africa, in April 1991 and reached Tangier, Morocco, at the beginning of September 1993. In this extract, she completed the initial stage of the journey with her first, rather awkward pair of drivers, Oli and Gerry. All three suffered from the 'moisture bees' the day before these drivers made their 'escape'.

E ach day I zig-zagged along the track, trying to find a firm base rather than trudging through soft sand. A trapped nerve in my back was sending shooting pains down my leg, but I was cheered up when I was joined by a gaggle of small children trotting to school. Wearing remnants of smart western clothes, they took an obvious delight in being around me and touching my hair. Walking on, I daydreamed of pulling the legs off croissants and of cold toast cut thinly and spread with *foie gras**.

A woman in a pink dress and wrap walked beside me, asking maternal questions and looking concerned. She told me her people were afraid of me but before she could explain, she hurried off, obviously afraid to be seen with

---

* *foie gras*: a very expensive goose-liver pâté

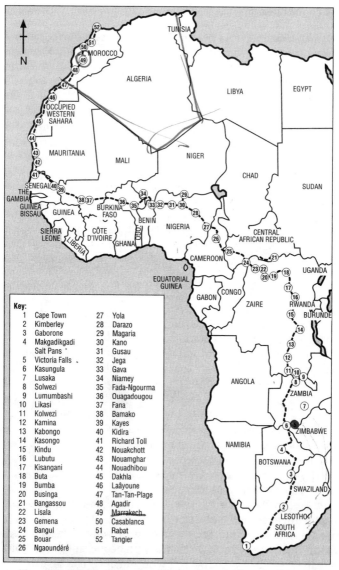

Key:

1	Cape Town	27	Yola
2	Kimberley	28	Darazo
3	Gaborone	29	Magaria
4	Makgadikgadi Salt Pans	30	Kano
		31	Gusau
5	Victoria Falls	32	Jega
6	Kasungula	33	Gava
7	Lusaka	34	Niamey
8	Solwezi	35	Fada-Ngourma
9	Lumumbashi	36	Ouagadougou
10	Likasi	37	Fana
11	Kolwezi	38	Bamako
12	Kamina	39	Kayes
13	Kabongo	40	Kidira
14	Kasongo	41	Richard Toll
15	Kindu	42	Nouakchott
16	Lubutu	43	Nouamghar
17	Kisangani	44	Nouadhibou
18	Buta	45	Dakhla
19	Bumba	46	Laâyoune
20	Businga	47	Tan-Tan-Plage
21	Bangassou	48	Agadir
22	Lisala	49	Marrakech
23	Gemena	50	Casablanca
24	Bangul	51	Rabat
25	Bouar	52	Tangier
26	Ngaoundéré		

Map showing the route that Ffyona Campbell took on her walk through Africa me. Soon afterwards I noticed that there were no footprints on the track. Where did the villagers walk? I left the road and 100 metres to the right, through thick bush, found a small track beside the remains of a railway. In places the metal line had been contorted by trees.

Where the path had been worn to soft sand, the locals had hacked another one, giving themselves firm footing for at least another few years. Woodsmoke hung like mist around the trees and the light streaming through made me feel safe. It was too thick to be made by cooking fires and there was no sign of life until I heard the distant beat of drums.

I tried to walk to the beat, but found it impossible. Instead my feet beat time with the throb of cicadas until I entered a beautiful village decorated with vines and brilliant red flowers that grew up the bamboo and brick-walled huts.

I had barely left the village outskirts when a swarm of flies attacked from nowhere. Swatting frantically and cursing, I wanted to run and hurl myself into water – anything to be free of them.

At lunchtime I arrived at the Land Rover and tore off my socks and shoes. They were covered with grass seeds that tore at my ankles and shins like rusty needle points. I didn't know what felt worse, the flies or the seeds.

I couldn't get away from either. Swatting frantically at the flies and cursing loudly, we made lunch in short time and consumed it in the sauna of the cab. While Oli danced around outside with first his rugby shirt over his head and then my mosquito net, Gerry lay beneath his net looking forlorn. Yet worse was to come.

The following evening, the flies were replaced by bees. A swarm descended before dusk as if defending their territory against interlopers. These insects were unusual. About half the size of a housefly, they don't sting, but swarm towards any moisture, whether it be the leaking lid of a jerry can or the perspiration on exposed skin. They dive into ears, mouths, and noses, crawling under shirt collars and cuffs and generally making life hell.

African bees get very dehydrated and crave water. We found the only way to distract them from the camp that night was by placing a washing-up bowl of water off in the bush. The swarm emptied it within a few hours.

For three days we were plagued by flies and moisture bees – driving me to the point of madness. During the wait for me, Oli and Gerry would cover up in mosquito nets, doubled over for extra protection, but still the bees would find a way through. The heat made it difficult to cover up against them. It was 38°C and felt like the inside of a laundromat tumble drier.

On our second-last night together before Lusaka, where Oli and Gerry were due to make their 'escape', we camped in a small village with a thirty-four-year-old local mechanic called Stanley who was named after the explorer. Stanley lived with his mother and grandparents and had spied the Land Rover and then later me and assumed it was a lovers' tiff which caused me to be walking.

We sat up late talking about the history and politics of Zambia. Stanley said it was hard for Zambians to feel any sense of nationalism because the borders of his country didn't correspond to any tribal or linguistic area: they had simply been imposed by the British. The region was called Northern Rhodesia until, after eleven years of fighting, they finally gained independence in 1964. But by this time much of Zambia's mineral wealth, mostly copper, had been mined and the money spent in Southern Rhodesia. It left the country in poverty. The diversity of the tribes was one reason why Dr Kaunda had formed a single, democratically elected, one-party government system. He used it to keep control and, since he was also the head of the armed forces, he effectively operated as a dictator. Much of Zambia's GNP was spent on supporting the anti-white terrorist parties in four neighbouring countries in their fight for independence, leaving citizens not only poor but highly suspicious of foreigners, who were seen as saboteurs or spies.

Stanley's grandmother moved a log further into the fire and settled back into the shadows. The smoke drew upwards and into the floor of the maize store above us where it dried the cobs, out of reach from rats. She'd heard Kaunda's name in conversation with these white strangers but she had faith in her grandson to protect her family.

Stanley told us of the forthcoming elections, where the villagers would have a chance to vote for a multi-party system. He, an educated man, didn't know what to believe, but, 'Anything is better than this.'

'Sounds familiar,' I said.

Stanley would make a point of voting but thousands of other villagers couldn't get to the polling stations. They had to work on their farms; they wouldn't walk for days to make their mark on a piece of paper which they didn't understand – and besides, what good would it do them? All they wanted was the freedom to live as they'd always done, but who cared enough to give them back their rights to hunt?

Stanley described how he had to hunt illegally – on his own land – using traps because they made no sound. He'd cut up the animal in the bush and bring back the meat, but he had to leave the skins, the bones, the sinews: everything, in fact, that was useful in case they were found in his village. They had to rely on commercial goods from larger village markets to replace those they could have made.

The following morning, Gerry and Oli sorted through their kit and gave Stanley his first pair of shoes. His mother got a sweatshirt and his grandparents had a pair of my sunglasses and a couple of pairs of socks. We shared our coffee and carried on our way.

The villages looked deserted as I walked through them, but I'd turn some way down the track and see the villagers standing there, watching me suspiciously. They'd return my wave, but almost as a spontaneous gesture before they realized what they were doing. Then I saw the Land Rover ahead, waiting for me and I thought, it will be better next time.

Oli had torn a dozen pages from his notebook and laid them in a line in the dirt, counting out my last steps to the Land Rover. He'd written a sign and pinned it to a tree: 'THE END. Lots of love from the boys. Good luck on the next stage.'

Travelling in Zaire, she found that villagers harassed her, suspecting that she was involved in slave trading. Her drivers on this second stage, Blake and Bill, were much more of a team than the previous pair, and would return along her route if she was late, in case the trouble had become serious.

We walked for several days until we reached Samba. All along that stretch we were continuously attacked on suspicion of being slave traders. I could do nothing to alleviate the harassment in the villages as they rejected even my smiles, the universal white flag. In their own environment, Africans are not desperate and despondent people as TV programmes often portray, they are courageous and they fight if they're scared. The Belgians were the worst of the colonials and they treated the Africans appallingly. The locals had long memories. If I had been French or Belgian I might not have got through. I kept my accent English and my grammar pidgin, which admittedly wasn't that difficult.

I was the constant focus of their attention. The boys went ahead through one village and I passed along ten minutes later to find the people still standing together in the centre staring after them. I came behind them, a white, undefended, feeling like a beetle walking into a dawn patrol of ants. An old man broke the silence with a barrage of shrill words. The crowd broke and re-formed around me, their shrill whooping getting louder and louder until it was a throbbing wall of sound. I daren't turn. I walked out of the village and I waved good-bye. Ten minutes later the hill behind was teeming with bands of children, whooping and hollering, their demands growing louder and louder. The tension needed relieving so I turned and smiled. They closed around me, getting excited. The ringleader grabbed at my necklace, demanding to know what it was.

'It is a present from my husband,' I said. 'Thank you for escorting me to him – he is waiting ahead.' And luckily both of them were.

Getting into camp was a relief not just because it meant I was safe but because I was not the only thing they were baiting any more.

A couple of boys would arrive first to watch the camp from a distance. Then more would come, just standing a small distance away. As the group grew, they merged into a crowd and became cocky. They were kids who'd found a new toy, and they loved to bait, to mess with it to see what it would do. They did this to me on the road – imitating me, shouting at me, and then a stone would be thrown. Blake had to defuse this in camp; I had to defuse this on the road. In camp, we could usually get them to leave in the early stages by picking out one and staring at him – this made them very self-conscious and they'd turn and leave.

On the road, I would turn around suddenly and growl with my hands out like claws. The children would scatter like impala changing direction. Some would take a look back at a distance and when they saw me laughing, they would laugh too and run back to hold my hand and dance along. But, after a short while, they wanted to do it again – as kids do – and the group would be gradually replaced as I walked through a long village, kids getting bored with it and falling back, to be replaced by new ones who started the baiting again.

The young teenage girls were the worst – they imitated my gait and would not respond to my games or return my smiles; they just sniggered. Teenage girls are the same the world over. There were times when I couldn't get the kids to laugh, possibly because I wasn't exuding the right presence. Then the stoning would be vicious. It is humiliating to be stoned, to be physically and symbolically chased out. I couldn't run; I couldn't stop them by stoning them back; I couldn't reason with them; I couldn't often get the adults to help. I was crying inside. Sometimes they hollered like Red Indians, a disorientating sound that made me feel like a hunted animal. I wondered if it was, indeed, a form of hunting. I hummed a Vangelis tune to make me feel like I wasn't actually there, just watching myself in a movie.

They read body language far better than us. They have grown up in a group and have learned to communicate more effectively without words – I think there are fewer misunderstandings. If I had been stoned in the last village and then saw different trees up ahead and knew there was another village coming, I would tense up. But I had to relax or face another stoning. I'd mull over something funny to make me laugh and relax my face muscles. I hated that first shrill call that signalled I'd been spotted, and mentally throttled the woman who'd made it.

I'd reply quickly in Swahili: 'Jambo Mama!' and walk over and shake her hand, clapping first.

The right hand is extended, the left is put on the crook of the right elbow. As a sign of respect to the elders, I would hold out my hand as a fist for my *wrist* to be shaken: this meant that I considered my hand too dirty to be shaken. When my fist was met by another fist for the first time, I was tempted to go into the scissor game.* You rub them together.

I would tell them I was walking for sport, that my husband was not far ahead. I always wore a wedding ring, a piece of advice given to me by Christina Dodwell, one of the greatest female explorers of our time. Sometimes they were very concerned for me, thinking I had been left behind by the Land Rover.

In Zaire, she had to abandon her walk temporarily and was evacuated home, with other foreigners, because war had broken out. She checked with the *Guinness Book of Records* that she could return and walk the missed section at a later date. These were some of her feelings as she finally reached the Mediterranean Sea, nearly two years after starting the African walk.

I was torn up inside. I didn't want this to end. I wanted the walking to end because I was tired, but I wanted to be like

* scissor game: a children's game

this always. I couldn't trade it in, I didn't want what was waiting for me after the beach. I didn't want to dance for sponsors or talk about my journey. I'd give them anecdotes of slave merchants, cannibals and evacuations, of missionaries and disease, lion tracks, tsetse fly and crossing minefields, but they couldn't have the private things.

A Short Walk in the Hindu Kush

Eric Newby

Eric Newby began his classic walk in the mountains of north-east Afghanistan aged 37 and with almost no preparation, apart from a few days walking in Snowdonia. His travelling life was a complete contrast with his previous work selling women's 'haute couture' clothes in a Mayfair fashion house. His friend Hugh Carless wrote to persuade him that the mountainous area was excellent walking country.

Hugh omitted to say much about the difficulty of provisioning an expedition or the dangers of being hit by falling boulders, although he knew about both problems from his recent experience in the area. Despite being unprepared, Eric not only completed the adventure, but went on to become a well-known expedition leader and travel writer. His books include *The Last Grain Race*, about crewing on a racing sailing ship, and *Slowly Down the Ganges,* a journey he took with his wife Wanda, travelling on a raft down the Indian holy river.

In this extract, Hugh and Eric have hired a team of Tajik tribesmen and baggage horses under the leadership of the impressive Abdul Ghiyas, who does not want to climb Mir Samir, the goal of the two travellers. Also with them was Badar Khan, whose kindness made life easier for the travellers.

A t six-thirty we arrived at the village of Marz Robat itself. We had been on the road for three hours and during this time had covered perhaps ten miles but, nevertheless, I felt utterly exhausted. By the look on Hugh's face he was experiencing somewhat similar sensations.

Outstripped by the *Mirgun** and his companion, whose opinions of our powers of locomotion were plain enough, we

---

* *Mirgun*: a man who has shot a thousand mountain goats

109

followed them into a narrow enclosure on the right of the road and sank down on the scruffy grass.

'You know,' said Hugh, 'I feel rather done up, I can't think why.'

'It must be the change of air.'

We were in a little garden high above the river, on the outskirts of the village, which belonged to a *chaie khana** across the road. The *chaie khana* was really only a hole in a wall with a sagging roof of dead vegetation strung on some long poles. Standing in a wooden cradle, looking like a medieval siege mortar and equally defunct, was a Russian samovar* made of copper and decorated with the Imperial eagles. It was splendid but unfortunately it was not working. Deciding that it would take a long time to get up a head of steam in a thing of this size, I closed my eyes in a coma of fatigue.

When I next opened them I was covered with a thick blanket of flies. They were somnolent in the cool of the evening and, when I thumped myself, squashing dozens of them, they simply rose a foot in the air and fell back on me with an audible 'plop', closing the ranks left by the slaughtered like well-drilled infantry.

Now the samovar was belching steam, jumping up and down on its wooden cradle in its eagerness to deliver the goods. It no longer resembled a cannon; it was more like an engine emerging from its shed anxious to be off up the line and away.

Bending over us was the proprietor, a curious-looking giant in a long brown cloak reaching to his feet, which stuck out coyly from under it. He was an object of nightmare but he brought with him all the apparatus of tea.

My teeth were chattering like castanets and without a word the giant took off his verminous cloak and wrapped me in it, leaving himself in a thin cotton shift. Another cloak was brought for Hugh. Here, when the sun went down, it was cold.

Regarding us silently from the walls of the little garden there was an immense audience. The male population of

* *chaie khana*: tea house   samovar: tea urn

Marz Robat, all but the bedridden, came to view these extraordinary beings who to them must have had all the strangeness of visitors from outer space. To appreciate their point of view one would have to imagine a Tajik stretched out in a garden in Wimbledon.

It was green tea and delicious but the cups were too small; pretty fine things of fine porcelain. After we had each drunk two entire pots we still had need of more liquid. Ours was not a thirst that proceeded from dry throats but a deep internal need to replace what had been sucked out of us in our unfit state by the power of the sun.

'I shouldn't do that,' Hugh croaked, as I demanded water. 'You'll be sorry.'

My powers of restraint, never great, had been broken. Now our roles were reversed.

'I thought you wanted me to drink it.'

'Not when you're tired. It's too cold.'

He was too late; the giant had already sent down to the river for a *chatti** of water. Somewhere I had read that salt was the thing for a person suffering from dehydration, so I called for salt too; a rock of it was produced and I put it in the pot, sluiced it round and drank deep. It was a nasty mixture but at least I felt that in some way I was justifying my lack of self-control.

All this time the crowd had been quietly slipping down off the wall and closing in on us; now they were all round us gorging with their eyes. We were the cynosure. Hugh was the first to crack.

'—!' He got up and stalked to the far end of the garden, tripping over his *chapan**. The crowd followed him but he barked at them so violently that they sheered off and settled on me.

With the intention of splitting them, I made for the only available corner (the other was occupied by the *Mirgun* and his friend), but as soon as I started to walk I found that there was something very wrong with my feet inside the Italian boots. It was as if a tram had gone over them. I sat

* *chatti*: can   *chapan*: flowing robe

down hastily, took the boots off and found that my socks were full of blood.

It seemed impossible that such damage could have been done in the space of three hours and some ten miles. My feet looked as though they had been flayed, as indeed they had.

How it had happened was a mystery; the boots were not tight, rather there was an excess of living-room inside them. The real trouble was that they were slightly pointed, whether because pointed shoes were the current Italian fashion and the designers thought that the appearance was improved or whether to facilitate rock climbing was not clear. What was certain was that for me pointed boots were excruciatingly painful.

Hugh tottered over to look and the villagers made little whistling sounds when they saw the extent of the damage. All of them knew the value of feet in the Hindu Kush. For some time Hugh said nothing. There was nothing to say and nothing to be done until Abdul Ghiyas arrived with the horses and the medicine chest.

'They're very bad,' he said at last. 'What do you want to do, go back to Kabul?'

To return to Kabul was useless; yet to go on seemed madness.

There was no question of my feet healing, the daily quota of miles would ensure that. I thought of all the difficulties we had overcome to get even as far as Marz Robat: the children uprooted from school; our flat let; my job gone; the money that Hugh and myself had expended; his own dotty dream of climbing Mir Samir to be frustrated at the last moment; my own dream, equally balmy, of becoming an explorer in the same way going up in smoke. I thought of the old inhabitant at Kabul. 'They're always setting off,' he had chuckled, 'that's as far as they get.' Were we to join this select body who had travelled only in their cups? There seemed to be no alternative but to go on. The fact that there was none rallied me considerably.

'We might be able to get you a horse,' Hugh said.

He could not have said anything better. I am completely ignorant of horses. The last time I had attempted to mount one I faced the wrong way when putting my foot in the stirrup and found myself in the saddle facing the creature's tail. Worse, being nervous of horses, I emanate a smell of death when close to them so that, sniffing it, they take fright themselves and attempt to destroy me. A horse would certainly have destroyed me on the road we had traversed that afternoon. At some places it had been only a couple of feet wide with a sheer drop to the river below.

'I think I'll carry on as I am. Another horse means another driver.'

'It would be *your* horse. We wouldn't need another driver.'

'If I walk they may harden up.' It was a phrase that I was to use constantly from now on.

It was fortunate that Abdul Ghiyas chose this moment to arrive with the rest of the party. Drivers and horses came lurching into the garden, all our gear banging against the stone walls in an alarming way. If this was what had been happening all along the road at the narrow places, most of it must have been shattered long ago.

All three were in a filthy temper, having been uprooted from their afternoon siesta and made to travel in the heat of the day. In an instant they cleared the garden of the crowds that milled about us and began to unload the horses, banging the boxes down like disgruntled housemaids and mumbling to themselves with averted eyes. It was not a propitious beginning to our life together.

'Are they always like this?' Watching this display of temperament I expressed my fears to Hugh.

'We haven't discussed terms with them yet. They're building themselves up for a good set-to about how much they're going to be paid. Then they'll quieten down a lot.'

'They're rather like *vendeuses*.* Can't we put them out of their misery?'

'You can't hurry things in this part of the world. They'll do it in their own way. Besides we don't want an audience. Wait until it gets dark. I should get on with dressing your feet.'

---

* *vendeuses*: fashion design sales asistant

As it grew dark Abdul Ghiyas moved all the equipment of the expedition close-in around us, hedging us with boxes and bundles so that we resembled ambushed settlers making a last stand. 'For fear of robbers,' as he put it. Within this enclosure we ate stewed apricots with lots of sugar, the only food that we could stomach in our debilitated condition. Almost at once, as Hugh had prophesied, we started to wrangle over wages.

'For the journey we offer thirty Afghanis a day. Also we will provide the food for your horses.' Hugh managed to make the part about the food sound like a benediction. At the bazaar rate of exchange thirty Afghanis is about four shillings.

The larger of the two drivers, whose name was Shir Muhammad, a surly-looking brute, said nothing but spat on the ground. To dispose of him at this delicate moment in the negotiations Hugh sent him to get sugar.

'Sugar, what do you want with sugar? If you come to our country why don't you live like us,' he mumbled, throwing the bag down in an ungracious way. 'This is a country of poor men.'

'What a noble animal is the horse,' said Abdul Ghiyas, striving to inject a more lofty note into a conversation that was in imminent danger of degenerating into an affair of mutual recrimination. 'The way is stony and hard for our horses. No man will take you to this mountain for thirty Afghanis a day.'

'... and food for the men,' said Hugh.

'That is the custom. Besides, who knows what perils Carless *Seb** will lead us into. Where will he take us after the mountain? Mir Samir is very close to Nuristan.'

'Thirty-five Afghanis.' Abdul Ghiyas had struck a subject that neither of us wanted to discuss at this stage. It was a shrewd thrust.

The silence that followed was so long that I began to think the discussion had lapsed completely.

---

* *Seb*: Sir

'The horse is the friend of man,' he said at last. 'The road is a difficult one. There are many perils on it, robbers and evil men. We are all married men. I am married, Shir Muhammad is married, Badar Khan is married ...' he indicated the smaller driver, the one with a thin moustache, who began to giggle.

'Forty Afghanis. Not one more.'

'Our children are numerous,' Shir Muhammad leered horribly. 'Who is to look after them when we are gone?'

'This is your own country. Surely you're not afraid of Tajiks.'

'There are Hazaras, heathen Shias ...'

'But the Hazaras of the Darra Hazara are your brothers, Sunnites.' This was one up to Hugh but Abdul Ghiyas ignored it.

'I have heard from the *mullah*[*] at Jangalak,' he went on, 'that only two days ago a Nuristani going down to Kabul to stay with his brother in the army was robbed of everything, his cloak too, by the Gujaras.'

I asked who the Gujaras were.

'Hill shepherds; partly nomad, from the Frontier, originally from the Punjab. There are some in Nuristan. They're semi-criminal – forty-five Afghanis.'

Finally, we settled for fifty Afghanis. Hugh grumbled a lot, 'don't know what the country's coming to', but to me it seemed remarkable that we had secured the services of three able-bodied men and their wiry little horses for the equivalent of six and eightpence each.

Now that all was concluded satisfactorily, the water pipe was circulated and Shir Muhammad heaped the fire with the fuel that the horses were producing at a greater rate than it could be consumed, an unusual experience for anyone used to living in Britain.

All night I was racked with pains in the stomach, the result of drinking water that was both ice-cold and dirty. Hugh, of course, was completely unaffected. Each time I got up I encountered Abdul Ghiyas. He was not asleep but

[*] *mullah*: Muslim preacher

squatting in the moonlight, ghostly in his white *chapan*, brooding over the kit, listening to the roar of the river.

A Traveller in China

Christina Dodwell

Christina Dodwell first began writing about her travels when she returned from three years riding a horse through Africa, a journey she began in 1975. Various methods of travelling appeal to different people and sometimes the terrain itself dictates the best type of transport to use. Christina Dodwell has also travelled on horseback through Turkey, which she wrote about in *A Traveller on Horseback*, and flown across West Africa in a microlight, a journey she recorded in *Travels with Pegasus*.

Here she tries another method of travel on Lake Karakol in China, 12,000 feet above sea level at the base of Mount Mustagh Ata. An earlier explorer Sven Hedin had almost drowned on the lake in 1894 in a boat made of poles and animal skins, and before she began to practise with hers, she had to break ice with her paddle. She got a lift back to town by road, but used the canoe later to shoot the rapids on the Yangtse river. The area she is travelling in here is across the Pamir mountain range from Eric Newby's explorations.

M y canoe, a French Sevylor craft, is streamlined and easily manoeuvrable, though I had to stop and collect a rock to hold down the nose. When its nose is too lightweight it doesn't steer well. Just for demonstration I paddled some tight figures of eight, though there was no one to be impressed, and raced myself from one side to the other. I liked the way that the turquoise colour of the water changed according to depth and to the state of the sky, which suddenly clouded over then came clear again. But Mustagh Ata was left engulfed, making its own clouds. Sven Hedin made several attempts to climb the mountain, but his best effort took him 3000 feet below the summit. Eric Shipton got to within 200 feet with Tilman in 1947, while he was British Consul General in Kashgar. For a while I watched and pondered Mustagh Ata's misty bulk, then turned and paddled back to the northern end to look for an exit stream leading towards Mount Kongur.

The river flowed out beneath moraine* so I carried the canoe until it became navigable. It coursed along a grassy valley and was split into several channels. My paddle hit the gravel bed sometimes and on turning shallow corners we bounced over pebbles. When I lifted my head I saw that all around were minor snowy peaks sloping down through barren sweeps into grassy valleys. Two tributaries swelled my stream, one from little Lake Karakol, and the larger from the glacier fields of Mustagh Ata and Kongur. Mount Kongur didn't seem to have any obvious peak; it is a hulking lumpy plateau with several summits jutting above its dark shield of ice-veined rock.

In 1980 the renowned climber Chris Bonington got permission to climb Mount Kongur, at the time the highest unclimbed peak in China. But Kongur proved a difficult challenge, made hazardous by avalanches and hidden crevasses, and near the top a storm forced his team to dig 'snow-coffins' in which they lay for three days and nights while the storm raged outside, before they reached the summit. The shape of a mountain can be as individual as a person's face, first seen as a distant two-dimensional image which looms up as it is approached, then vanishing and coming back into sight as one meanders through its buttressing ridges and forked valleys. Mountains have a multi-faceted nature that is gradually revealed by observation from different points. Each point of view brings new understanding. Longer communing with a mountain brings a special significance. Later when the mountain recedes into the distance, it will be recognizable even as an undistinguished peak in a horizon of mountains.

A snow-storm blew up. Seeing some huts not far from the river, I went to seek shelter and was offered a cup of tea by the Kirghiz family living there. The tea was brewed with sheep's milk and the stove was fuelled by dried sheep's droppings. From the stove the woman took a freshly-baked

---

* moraine: debris from a glacier

Christina Dodwell – her journeys have taken her to Africa, beyond Siberia, across Turkey and Iran, to China and Papua New Guinea

bread-cake; it was delicious. The man of the house was ill, he had a fever but he had been seen and treated by a doctor. I spent a short time in conversation with him. He was not a poor man, he owned 25 sheep, two horses, some yaks and two camels. Near his stone and mud hut was a round felt yurt,* the children said their grandmother lived there, and took me to meet her. From behind the heavy felt curtain, which acted as a front door, there was strung a mysterious long woven strip of material which stretched some way outside and its end was pegged to the ground.

We called out and the children pushed aside the curtain for me to enter. The yurt's interior was spacious, warm from the stove and thick felt walls, and airy because of a large circular opening in the roof. The old lady was working at a tripod-shaped loom, nimbly weaving more of the long woollen strip in a blend of red, yellow and green. A calf and a baby goat were resting in a section partitioned off for them.

When the storm abated I said my goodbyes, collected the canoe which I had tied to the yurt, and returned to the river which followed Kongur's base for about two miles and gathered water from three glaciers. The vast size of the mountain filled the whole of my eastern horizon. It made me feel as insignificant as an ant or a particle of sand. The watercourse flowed through an area of prickly scrub, less than a yard tall but spikier than a coil of barbed wire. I wondered if it is the type of sand millet whose seeds can be made into flour, and maybe baked into the type of cake that I'd just eaten. People don't try to touch the spiky bush, they just put a cloth underneath and hit it with sticks until the grains fall.

Still meandering in many shallow channels, I grated over pebbles a couple of times and nearly got snagged on some prickly branches which had fallen into the water. Later I did notice that a little air was escaping from one tube of the canoe but it could only have been a pinprick and it stayed afloat well enough. As I approached a U-bend the

---

* yurt: a type of tent

current began pushing the canoe too close to a bank overhung with prickles. I steered away but the current steered more strongly. With growing alarm I directed the canoe across the river, straining to get away from the bank. The canoe suddenly responded, shooting us into the shallows, now broadside to the stream. Trying to swing the nose straight I hit a rock, the canoe bounced off it and straightened up backwards. Now facing the wrong way, I looked over my shoulder and realized that the river was growing quickly narrower. For some harrowing moments I paddled cautiously, twisting around to see what we were in for. Another bend loomed, I couldn't manage it in reverse, the movements are back to front. My confidence plummeted and I misjudged it. We hit a sandy piece of cliff which crumbled down on to the spraydeck cover, but in that moment I had space to spin the nose downriver. Awkwardly achieved, but at least I was now facing forward again.

From Kongur's base the river descended into barren scenery, under an iron roadbridge and down a deceptively swift stretch where the water looked a milky blue colour. The weather began to get worse, there was strong wind and a few snowflakes. I hurried for several miles until the clouds cleared away to the south, leaving me in an area of silvery white sand mountains, their shape eroded into flowing curves which glistened in the cold sunlight. The beauty there was something special. Perhaps it was enhanced by being so little known and untraversed. The river spread again into a series of ponds; a marshland of sedge-tussocks. The chains of pools grew so shallow that I portaged around them and put in again where the river became deep. It was at the beginning of a gorge. Its barren sides grew taller and its course was made rough by boulders, but there was nothing threatening and I thoroughly enjoyed learning to handle my canoe. So far I had stayed fairly dry, the spraydeck covers at front and back were effective and my small bag of luggage was tucked down by my legs. Steering and driving the canoe with a double-bladed paddle is certainly simpler than using a wooden one-bladed type.

Another blizzard blew up and since it was late in the day I stopped as soon as I found a hut where I could shelter. It was a cold but uneventful night, and the next day began with that crystal sunshine you only find at high altitudes. The air was as crisp and pure as the cry of a falcon. By mid-morning I'd gone through a section of brown shale mountains, seeming bleached of all colour. Bare rock, sometimes banded with whites and reds, and no plants except sparse spiky brush. And beyond it all, the icy peaks and glaciers.

The river grew steeper but because it wasn't in flood, it poured evenly over ledges and down over boulder obstacles in fairly gentle chutes. The canoe bucked its way through them, but at one chute I hit a boulder at the wrong angle. Suddenly we tipped sideways. I shoved my paddle-blade against another rock to push myself upright, the blade slipped and, dropping the paddle, I reached out to fend us off by hand. It worked, but the paddle was gone. Anxiously scanning the water I saw it nearby and managed to paddle with my hands and retrieve it. Fortunately at this point the river was not fast, and although there were some long, semi-turbulent stretches, they looked rougher than they really were. At one of the quieter pools I stopped to have a short rest and munch on some of the dried food that I still carried. It was rather idyllic. I doubted that the river had ever been run before, since for most of the year it's swollen and totally unnavigable. But being the first wasn't important, I wasn't trying to achieve anything. I just wanted to try out my canoe. The voyage wouldn't be a long one, just a day or so, since the river's lower course near Kashgar, which goes through endless flat wheat fields, didn't interest me.

Some tribesmen on horseback caught sight of me, their horses muffled up in blankets and the men in woolly coats and hats. One was carrying a baby yak across his saddle. I waved but they had already spurred their steeds and were hurrying away along the track halfway up the gorge. The only person I spoke to was an old herdsman and during our conversation he mentioned that some relatives of his had been Chris Bonington's porters to Mount Kongur. The herdsmen had taken their oldest and sickest yaks on the trip, hoping that they would die, because although the pay wasn't much, the Chinese government had promised compensation for any yaks that died on the expedition.

The river had cut its gorge through different rock strata, and from shale I entered a conglomerate area with large pebbles embedded in rock. There didn't seem to be any arable land. The sparse dwellings blended into the scenery so well (being made of the same materials) that they were almost invisible. From one bank I spotted a group of beehive-shaped huts. Often I got out of the canoe to reconnoitre along the bank, and if necessary to lift the canoe around an impassable rapid, but I was unprepared for disaster when it struck.

An innocent ledge jettisoned the canoe into a barrage of rocks and a maelstrom current which pushed me back into a trough of churning water at the bottom of the ledge. Water flooded into the canoe. I was petrified and the shock of the icy water pouring over me nearly immobilized me. I tried to paddle free but the paddle blades kept hitting rocks. Then as we came clear, the canoe reared up against a partly submerged rock and to my horror I was overturned. My hands scrabbled at the slippery rocks, anything to get out of the freezing water, but I could get no hold. So I floundered toward the bank, gasping with fright, swimming a rapid in the process but without injury, and got washed up on the shore. My canoe was still in the river, ahead of me, and forgetting my numbness I charged after it. It jammed across a rapid then went through. I ran for all I was worth. Fortunately it stuck again against some rocks and I was able to grab its rope and pull it on to the shore. The paddle arrived in its wake. For a moment I lay coughing up water on the ground beside the canoe, then kicked myself into action again. The cold was intense and I shivered uncontrollably while I emptied the canoe of water and righted its contents. Everything was wet but nothing important was missing.

In some ways I wanted to stop my canoe journey then and there, but a small voice inside me said that I should paddle on at least until reaching a good place to climb out of the gorge and rejoin the road. Despite my wet clothes and miserable state, my spirits picked up again as I continued downriver. It would be hard to stay depressed in such magnificent landscape. Red rocky mountains towered above the craggy grey gorge. But within a short distance I started shaking with cold and decided to abandon the river. It was late afternoon. After deflating and packing away my canoe I got a lift back to Kashgar in an army truck. As we came down to the lowlands and out between red cliffs I glanced behind and saw some of the peaks I had passed earlier, now receding into the distance.

Journey through Europe

John Hillaby

John Hillaby has made several walking journeys, in Britain, America and Africa. In *Journey through Love*, one of his later travel books, he journeyed through Britain and across the Appalachian Trail in North America, in order to ease the grief of his wife's death. His usual way of travelling is on foot, but in this extract, from *Journey through Europe,* he makes it clear that he is not a mountaineer. He has tried several times to cross the *col de Bonhomme*, a mountain pass, but given up after floundering in snow for some while.

It seems clear that the young Frenchmen he meets in an Alpine hut just below the *col,* do not mean the same thing by 'walk' as he does. He realizes rather late that same night some of the more subtle shades of meaning in French, but even if the threesome are not conversationalists, the Frenchmen are generous in assisting him over the highest point of his climb. They may not be great talkers, but all three become exhibitionists in the exhilaration of the snow. John Hillaby is helped to continue over the Alps to complete his journey through Italy, down to the warmth of the French coast.

The mountaineers looked up with no surprise. I didn't expect an uproarious welcome, but felt that the sudden appearance of a snow-sprinkled fellow-traveller at the door of La Balme, the mountain hut below the *col de Bonhomme*, merited something more than a muttered *'Ça va?'** from the more eloquent of the two. His companion nodded and went on reading the tablecloth, an old copy of the *Journal de Genève.*

As for myself, I had had more than ample time to rehearse introductions since I had looked down on that little hut for more than three hours.

* *Ça va?*: 'How's things?'

It lies on the GR5, some three or four miles above Les
Contamines, a refuge on the first platform of a bleak pass.
With the sky bright and the air crisp, all seemed set for a
solo assault. But though I tried and tried hard to get over
that *col* by three different routes, it literally beat me flat. I
fell on my face twice. I couldn't make any headway. A
repetition of the Anterne venture. The track lay buried
beneath a *cirque** of snow, quite soft on the floor of the cleft,
but in places deep. I tackled the rocks on the rim; I
floundered about on the slopes. After an unnerving and
wholly unpremeditated *glissade** head-first into a drift, I
slunk back to the hut convinced that nobody could get
through without snow-shoes or skis.

All this I intended to relate in studied understatement to
whoever inhabited the hut. I had seen a tent near the door.
But something about the two young men recommended
caution. Their ice-axes looked very professional. They were
out for a walk, they said. Not to be outdone by this show of
Gallic nonchalance, I said I had been doing a bit myself,
trying to give the impression I had merely been up to the
col to see what it looked like.

Henri and Alain were making the *Tour de Mont Blanc,*
keeping to the trail that winds round the whole *massif** by
way of Entrèves, La Fouly, the Forclaz, Montroc and the *col
du Brevent,* a brisk nine days' walk around as many
glaciers in a range of light. They knew the *Bonhomme*
pretty well, they said. They usually went over it once or
twice a year. Sometimes they scrambled over Mont Tondu,
but that week they intended to take it easy, starting with
the *col* the next morning.

'At what time?'

'Half past four.'

'Why so early?'

'To see the sun rise,' said Henri.

A cool pair. Friendly but not given to small-talk. The
tradition is that, more than any other race, the British are
particularly reticent among strangers, but less so, I think,

---

* *cirque*: deep, round hollow   *glissade*: slide   *massif*: range of mountains

than young Frenchmen with the disconcerting habit of answering questions in two or three words. The two came from Lyons. No, they said, they didn't work there. They designed reactors at Pierrelatte, the atomic centre. A good place to escape from. As for themselves they came to Savoy to get away from people.

* * *

We British are a sensitive race. For the better part of an hour I sat in a corner deciphering a dull article on the Common Market in the *Journal de Genève.*

Dark came down, coldly. It began to snow. Henri and Alain yawned and made for the door. They slept outside, saying it felt warmer and more comfortable in a tent. I pitched mine alongside, and they were both snoring exuberantly before I managed to work out that remark about getting away from people.

Henri woke me with a mug of hot coffee and a thimbleful of *marc**. By the time I had packed and crawled out into the pale blue light, they were waiting. Although they carried a tent and cooking gear, my pack seemed twice the size of their own. '*Formidable*,' said Alain, lifting it up gingerly. 'Where is your *piolet*?' I didn't know what he meant. He tapped his ice-axe. I had no *piolet*, I said.

We walked together, rapidly, over a thin powdering of snow. When it became deep, the uncommunicative Alain took the lead. He mounted a steep slope at right angles to the floor of the *col*, and struck out along a barely discernible ridge.

At first they affected to ignore my performance as a person might charitably look aside when his partner fluffs a golf shot or miscues at billiards. For a time they may have thought they were in the company of somebody who had evolved a new technique of tackling snow slopes by digging his heels in. If so, they were quickly disillusioned. Whilst they trudged forward resolutely, step by step, scarcely altering their pace however steep the traverse, I floundered

---

* *marc*: a kind of brandy

and slipped. At one point I tried to scramble back to the ridge on all fours. It soon became clear I didn't know a thing about how to walk on snow.

Henri showed me how to dig my toes in so that I trod deep, impelled by my own momentum. He advised me to keep close so that when he began to chop steps, usually with a single stroke of his axe, I had something firm to put my feet on. I kept my eyes on those steps, scarcely daring to look down the appalling sweep of the slope below, but when, to give me confidence, Alain handed me his own *piolet*, the feeling of acute nausea passed and I merely felt chronically giddy. My instructors were patient and highly professional.

Dawn broke. Clouds as delicate as the tails of egrets glowed and caught fire in the first great shafts of light from the east. Peak after peak appeared around Mont Pourri in the Vanoise. With its white walls and rose-coloured roof that great dome looked like the pavilion of a chief among the tents of his men. The light also disclosed shameful evidence of what I had done wrong the previous day.

Far below my footprints stood out as if some distracted creature had scampered about, trying to avoid some threat from above which, I suppose, is more or less what it amounted to. The tracks wavered about uncertainly, and at the point where I lost my balance and rolled over they ended in a long blue-grey smudge. Observing merely that it must have been an experience, Henri threw back his head and began to yodel, invoking a series of echoes from the crags around.

About high mountain air in the morning there is a super-tonic quality. It confounds that pompous stuff called human gravity, which, as somebody put it, serves only to conceal the defects of the mind. Any reticence there might have been between us blew away. We joked and fell about each other, throwing snowballs. Alain sang barrack-room songs and Henri whirled down a slope in the manner of a *ramasseur**.

---

* *ramasseur*: a ball boy on a tennis-court

To perform that feat you sit on your heels and push off, using your *piolet* as a handbrake. He carried out some remarkable acrobatics culminating in a series of broad loops, controlled at speed by digging his axe in at full arm's length. When I tried to do the same I succeeded only in rolling over again, breaking another rivet in the frame of my rucksack. After much of this we struck out for the second ridge, the *Croix de Bonhomme.*

I have often thought about setting off for a long walk in the company of one or two friends, but, with cautionary memories of a few sailing trips, I have never actually tried it. Toleration for the close and prolonged company of all but a few intimates tends to diminish progressively until you can't bear the way somebody drums his fingers or repeats an irritating little phrase. But at the beginning, before the hard corners of mannerisms and personality begin to stick out, all is conviviality. We go out of our way to show what companionable fellows we are, and so it was with us that morning. We swopped addresses and bits of chocolate. I gladly sacrificed a quarter of brandy bought only for the most dire of emergencies. We told tales of what we recalled most vividly and since the two were for climbing rather than walking, my stock of adventure in lonely places seemed meagre besides their own especially on the subject of storms, for on one occasion they had actually been struck by lightning.

As Henri described the incident, they had climbed up to a high ledge in winter, determined on reaching a *réfuge* in the *col de Chavannes*. It became overcast. Fearing snow, they climbed rapidly, cutting deep steps, hauling themselves up steep places by using their axes as *grappins,* that is as anchors or grapnels to which they tied their ropes. On one ledge they put an extra heavy strain on an axe that began to emit a high-pitched whine, 'like a bee'. As if in sympathy, the other axe started to whine in the same way. This is the song of the ice-axe, *la chanson du piolet,* an electrostatic effect that occurs when the atmosphere is heavily charged.

Suddenly, all at a blow, they were deafened as a discharge struck at the lightning conductor dangling from the ledge. The two men were thrown into the snow. They weren't hurt, but they felt completely numb, *engourdi* as they put it, and they lost about thirty metres of rope. It didn't burn up. The fibres opened and they were left with a few handfuls of fluff and the charred shaft of one of their axes. 'Down from that place we came like rabbits,' said Henri.

When I look back I consider that brief stage as the high point in what little I have learned about walking through snow-covered places. Without it, I doubt if I could have got through what came later, but it seemed nothing but pleasurable at the time. If Henri and Alain remember those four or five hours between La Balme and the Cross of the Good Fellow, it will be, I hope, with amusement. We parted on the cliffs of Les Chapieux. They were making for the Miage glacier. I had a less appealing appointment in Bourg St Maurice with some television people from London.

A Thousand Miles up the Nile

Amelia Edwards

Amelia Edwards was born in 1831 and grew up writing poems and articles for magazines. By 1881 she had also written eight novels. Aged 42, single and bored with getting wet whilst travelling in Europe with a friend, she decided they should arrange their own voyage up the Nile. At the time, Thomas Cook had just begun to organize tours which were to become the earliest of package holidays, but Amelia wanted to arrange her own trip and often compared her experience with that of the early Cook's tourist.

Her first and very difficult task in Cairo was the hiring of a dahabeeyah, a flat-bottomed wooden boat at the right price, size and comfort for herself, her friend and their maid. All this had to be done without a common language between the crew and the customer. Finally, she persuaded four other Europeans (including honeymooners she refers to as the Happy Couple) to share a comfortable large dahabeeyah with them, along with the costs, and the crew. Their boat was named the Philae after one of Egypt's most beautiful temples, and she thought it 'not very unlike the Noah's Ark of our childhood'.

The crew included a cook and a dragoman (interpreter) called Talhamy, and sitting on the upper deck which served as an open-air sitting room, the party of travellers set off upstream to the sound of a six-gun salute as the Philae set sail. At the first stop their small group was mistaken for a Cook's tour and the villagers were most disappointed that only eight donkeys were needed.

Their stay at Assûan (modern Aswan), where the Nile flows around Elephantine island, gave her time to sample another way of travelling.

But for the impressionable traveller, the Assûan camel is *de rigueur*[*]. In his interest are those snarling quadrupeds be-tasselled and berugged, taken from their regular work, and paraded up and down the landing-place. To transport cargoes disembarked above and below the Cataract is their vocation. Taken from this honest calling to perform in an absurd little drama got up especially for the entertainment of tourists, it is no wonder if the beasts are more than commonly ill-tempered. They know the whole proceeding to be essentially cockney, and they resent it.

The ride, nevertheless, has its advantages; not the least being that it enables one to realize the kind of work involved in any of the regular desert expeditions. At all events, it entitles one to claim acquaintance with the ship of the desert, and (bearing in mind the probable inferiority of the specimen) to form an *ex pede* judgement of his qualifications.

The camel has his virtues – so much at least must be admitted; but they do not lie upon the surface. My Buffon tells me, for instance, that he carries a fresh-water cistern in his stomach; which is meritorious. But the cistern ameliorates neither his gait nor his temper – which are abominable. Irreproachable as a beast of burden, he is open to many objections as a steed. It is unpleasant, in the first place, to ride an animal which not only objects to being ridden, but cherishes a strong personal antipathy to his rider. Such, however, is his amiable peculiarity. You know that he hates you, from the moment you first walk round him, wondering where and how to begin the ascent of his hump. He does not, in fact, hesitate to tell you so in the roundest terms. He swears freely while you are taking your seat; snarls if you but move in the saddle; and stares you angrily in the face, if you attempt to turn his head in any direction save that which he himself prefers. Should you persevere, he tries to bite your feet. If biting your feet does not answer, he lies down.

Now the lying-down and getting-up of a camel are performances designed for the express purpose of inflicting

[*] *de rigueur*: obligatory

grievous bodily harm upon his rider. Thrown twice forward and twice backward, punched in his 'wind' and damaged in his spine, the luckless novice receives four distinct shocks, each more violent and unexpected than the last. For this 'execrable hunchback' is fearfully and wonderfully made. He has a superfluous joint somewhere in his legs, and uses it to revenge himself upon mankind.

His paces, however, are more complicated than his joints and more trying than his temper. He has four: – a short walk, like the rolling of a small boat in a chopping sea; a long walk which dislocates every bone in your body; a trot that reduces you to imbecility; and a gallop that is sudden death. One tries in vain to imagine a crime for which the *peine forte et dure** of sixteen hours on camel-back would not be a full and sufficient expiation. It is a punishment to which one would not willingly be the means of condemning any human being – not even a reviewer.

They had been down on the bank for hire all day long – brown camels and white camels, shaggy camels and smooth camels; all with gay worsted tassels on their heads, and rugs flung over their high wooden saddles, by way of housings. The gentlemen of the Fostât* had ridden away hours ago, cross-legged and serene; and we had witnessed their demeanour with mingled admiration and envy. Now, modestly conscious of our own daring, we prepared to do likewise. It was a solemn moment when, having chosen our beasts, we prepared to encounter the unknown perils of the desert. What wonder if the Happy Couple exchanged an affecting farewell at parting?

We mounted and rode away; two imps of darkness following at the heels of our camels, and Salame* performing the part of bodyguard. Thus attended, we found ourselves pitched, swung, and rolled along at a pace that carried us rapidly up the slope, past a suburb full of cafés and grinning dancing girls, and out into the desert. Our way for the first half-mile or so lay among the tombs.

---

* *peine forte et dure* : long, drawn-out misery
  Fostât : another boatload of travellers
  Salame : one of their crew

The travellers rode on to the great granite quarries of Assûan, in particular to see the almost-finished obelisk which would have been the largest in the world. As the workmen undercut the huge stone, destined to become a pharaoh's monument, they discovered the granite was flawed. They left it where it still rests today.

Like many contemporary travellers, the group wanted to watch the sun go down from a hilltop nearby.

And now, there being still an hour of daylight, we signified our intention of making for the top of the nearest hill, in order to see the sun set. This, clearly, was an unheard-of innovation. The camel-boys stared, shook their heads, protested there was 'mafeesh sikkeh' (no road), and evidently regarded us as lunatics. The camels planted their splay feet obstinately in the sand, tried to turn back, and, when obliged to yield to the force of circumstances, abused us all the way. Arrived at the top, we found ourselves looking down upon the island of Elephantine, with the Nile, the town, and the dahabeeyahs at our feet. A prolongation of the ridge on which we were standing led, however, to another height crowned by a ruined tomb; and seemed to promise a view of the Cataract. Seeing us prepare to go on, the camel-boys broke into a *furore** of remonstrance, which, but for Salame's big stick, would have ended in downright mutiny. Still we pushed forward, and, still dissatisfied, insisted on attacking a third summit. The boys now trudged on in sullen despair. The sun was sinking; the way was steep and difficult; the night would soon come on. If the Howadji* chose to break their necks, it concerned nobody but themselves; but if the camels broke theirs, who was to pay for them?

Such – expressed half in broken Arabic, half in gestures – were the sentiments of our youthful Nubians. Nor were the camels themselves less emphatic. They grinned; they sniffed; they snorted; they snarled; they disputed every foot

* *furore* : an uproar Howadji: foreigners

of the way. As for mine (a gawky, supercilious beast with a bloodshot eye and a battered Roman nose), I never heard any dumb animal make use of so much bad language in my life.

The last hill was very steep and stony; but the view from the top was magnificent. We had now gained the highest point of the ridge which divides the valley of the Nile from the Arabian desert. The Cataract, widening away reach after reach and studded with innumerable rocky islets, looked more like a lake than a river. Of the Libyan desert we could see nothing beyond the opposite sand-slopes, gold-rimmed against the sunset. The Arabian desert, a boundless waste edged by a serrated line of purple peaks, extended eastward to the remotest horizon. We looked down upon it as on a raised map. The Moslem tombs, some five hundred feet below, showed like toys. To the right, in a wide valley opening away southwards, we recognized that ancient bed of the Nile which serves for the great highway between Egypt and Nubia. At the end of the vista, some very distant palms against a rocky background pointed the way to Philae.

Their next stop was indeed the temple of Philae, but to get there, travellers on the Nile had to have their boats hauled up the rapids known as 'the Cataracts'. Since the Aswan Dam was built, the river has been tamed but for the group on board in 1873, it was an adventure that nearly became a tragedy. The Sheykh or Lord of the Cataract governed the sailors who hauled the dahabeeyahs – and it was only after a night's worry and the Sheykh's extra 'force of two hundred men' that the *Philae* got under way again.

The scenery of the First Cataract is like nothing else in the world – except the scenery of the Second. It is altogether new, and strange, and beautiful. It is incomprehensible that travellers should have written of it in general with so little admiration. They seem to have been impressed by the wildness of the waters, by the quaint forms of the rocks, by the desolation and grandeur of the landscape as a whole; but scarcely at all by its beauty – which is paramount.

The Nile here widens to a lake. Of the islands, which it would hardly be an exaggeration to describe as some hundreds in number, no two are alike. Some are piled up like rocks at the Land's End in Cornwall, block upon block, column upon column, tower upon tower, as if reared by the hand of man. Some are green with grass; some golden with slopes of drifted sand; some planted with rows of blossoming lupins, purple and white. Others again are mere cairns of loose blocks, with here and there a perilously balanced top-boulder. On one, a singular upright monolith, like a menhir, stands conspicuous, as if placed there to commemorate a date, or to point the way to Philae. Another mass rises out of the water squared and buttressed, in the likeness of a fort. A third, humped and shining like the wet body of some amphibious beast, lifts what seems to be a horned head above the surface of the rapids. All these blocks and boulders and fantastic rocks are granite; some red, some purple, some black. Their forms are rounded by the friction of ages. Those nearest the brink reflect the sky like mirrors of burnished steel. Royal ovals and hieroglyphed inscriptions, fresh as of yesterday's cutting, start out here and there from those glittering surfaces with startling distinctness. A few of the larger islands are crowned with clumps of palms; and one, the loveliest of any, is completely embowered in gum-trees and acacias, dôm and date palms, and feathery tamarisks, all festooned together under a hanging canopy of yellow-blossomed creepers.

* * *

At length a general stir among the crew warned us of the near neighbourhood of the first rapid. Straight ahead, as if ranged along the dyke of a weir, a chain of small islets barred the way; while the current, divided into three or four headlong torrents, came rushing down the slope, and reunited at the bottom in one tumultuous race.

That we should ever get the *Philae* up that hill of moving water seemed at first sight impossible. Still our steersman held on his course, making for the widest channel. Still the Sheykh smoked imperturbably. Presently, without removing the pipe from his mouth, he delivered the one word – 'Roóhh!' (Forward!)

Instantly, evoked by his nod, the rocks swarmed with natives. Hidden till now in all sorts of unseen corners, they sprang out shouting, gesticulating, laden with coils of rope, leaping into the thick of the rapids, splashing like water-dogs, bobbing like corks, and making as much show of energy as if they were going to haul us up the Niagara. The thing was evidently a *coup de théâtre*, like the apparition of Clan Alpine's warriors in the Donna del Lago – with backshîsh* in the background.

The scene that followed was curious enough. Two ropes were carried from the dahabeeyah to the nearest island, and there made fast to the rocks. Two ropes from the island were also brought on board the dahabeeyah. A double file of men on deck, and another double file on shore, then ranged themselves along the ropes; the Sheykh gave the signal; and, to a wild chanting accompaniment and a movement like a barbaric Sir Roger de Coverley dance, a system of double hauling began, by means of which the huge boat slowly and steadily ascended. We may have been a quarter of an hour going up the incline; though it seemed much longer. Meanwhile, as they warmed to their work, the men chanted louder and pulled harder, till the boat went in at last with a rush, and swung over into a pool of comparatively smooth water.

Having moored here for an hour's rest, we next repeated the performance against a still stronger current a little higher up. This time, however, a rope broke. Down went the haulers, like a row of cards suddenly tipped over – round swung the *Philae,* receiving the whole rush of the current

---

* backshîsh: a tip

on her beam! Luckily for us, the other rope held fast against the strain. Had it also broken, we must have been wrecked then and there ignominiously.

People's ideas

People use writing to express their heartfelt views about the world and the people living in it. The writer may make us laugh, feel angry, make us change our opinions, or tell us things that widen our understanding of the world.

Issues such as starvation, social injustice, education, the relationship between the sexes, our care for the world around us make journalists over the centuries take up their pens or switch on word-processors. Foreign correspondents travel the world to bring us their accounts of wars and revolutions, which we then see on our TV screens and read in our newspapers. There is a real hunger amongst us to know about the world we live in and many people earn a living by supplying us with information. Much of this material quickly becomes out-of-date and it is difficult to know what will disappear almost without trace, and what will have lasting value.

We can find out a great deal about past and recent events through reading journalists' accounts. However, we need to remember that each writer can only witness a part of the 'story' and will hold a personal view of events.

Examinations

Polly Toynbee

Polly Toynbee writes regularly for *The Guardian* and reviews programmes for *Radio Times*. She often turns her attention to educational matters and here writes about an issue which you may have views on yourself. As you read her suggestions, you may find yourself agreeing with some of them. Is 'free to do nothing' the way you would like to spend a school day?

If we really want to do something dramatic to improve the lives of our children for this International Year of the Child, we should free their childhood from exams and selection.

At the tender age of thirteen or fourteen children are thrust into GCSE classes that will, to all intents and purposes, seal their futures. Then, at the age in their lives when most of them are least receptive to learning, they are forced to sit exams where the penalties for failure are truly momentous.

The lives of secondary school children are dominated by these exams. Parents continue to push, pull, bully and worry their children through exams, or search anxiously for schools with 'high standards' to do the pushing and bullying for them, because that is what our universities demand.

But is there any need for all that? What's the hurry? The labour market is not exactly crying out for very young newly qualified people. Why do we put such pressure on our adolescents? What do they want? Between the ages of thirteen and sixteen a great many adolescents feel less like studying and learning than at any other time in their lives. The business of growing up is enough. For a lot of the time nothing preoccupies their minds, or they are busy coming to terms with sex, God and socialism. They need time, and space. Often highly motivated children who have read libraries of books suddenly come to a stop at adolescence. It doesn't mean they'll stop forever. With any luck after about sixteen or seventeen they come out of that phase, but under our present system, that's too late. If they took the wrong course at fourteen, then they've had their chips. Parents can easily despair at children who given the chance spend half the day in bed, and the other half getting dressed, but it doesn't last for ever. So why do we choose this period in their lives as the time to make or break them?

If the pressures of selection at sixteen were removed, secondary education could become a different process altogether. From about thirteen onwards children should be free to study if they choose, as obsessively as they like. Or they could choose to study part of the time. They could spend exactly as long as they wanted doing the subjects they wanted to do. Or otherwise they would be free to do nothing. Schools would have sitting space for them to do nothing in. If they wanted to spend half of the day in the art rooms, or doing drama that would be their decision. Since the 1930s such progressive schools have existed, but while the present exam system exists, the penalties for encouraging a child to develop its own interests and talents and not satisfy matriculation requirements can be severe.

To torment and terrify recalcitrant adolescents with threats of failure seems to me a scarcely better way to teach than the old methods of beating education into them.

When I consider that between the ages of five and eighteen at school I was subjected to 17,745 lessons at a time when the brain is biologically at its most receptive, and how little I knew at the end of it all, I am astounded by the waste of time, money and effort. The school day itself is hardly conducive to teaching serious application and concentration, divided up into those arbitrary 40-minute gobbets of learning. Classes shunt along school corridors like cars on a conveyor belt to have a bit of French welded on here, and a bit of geography there, a rivet of algebra hammered on top of a nugget of community studies.

Children bear the brunt of the whole society's aspirations. Standards in education is such an emotive subject because we invest our sense of identity and success in how many A grades at A level the nation can squeeze out of its children. If they do badly then hysterical statements get tossed around the Houses of Parliament declaring that society is rotten, decadent, collapsing. If we are assured that children are still being sufficiently battered with theorems, ablative absolutes, and dates, people breathe easier and feel that society is still on its feet. Ultimately, of course we do have to turn out plenty of highly educated people, but we don't have to cram reluctant adolescents in order to do so. People can learn later, when they are more able and willing to do so.

Most children cannot concentrate under these oppressive conditions. The very act of being taught all day by people who know better is enough to make any but the most highly motivated rebel. The only point of the system is that it makes organizational and administrative sense but it can hardly be called efficient. Why, for instance, does it take five years of lessons to get children up to a paltry GCSE standard in French? If someone really wanted to teach an eleven-year-old French and the child actually wanted to learn, it could be done in a matter of months.

The voice of the children themselves is rarely heard, and all too often, when they do write about education, they merely parrot what their teachers and parents have said. But one clear, articulate and reasoned view comes from the National Union of School Students.

John Munford, one of the NUSS's two full-time organizers, is sixteen and has just left a Harlech comprehensive. He is now studying for his A levels in London at the same time as working for the NUSS.

The NUSS is still in its infancy, with a membership of only 10,000 and an income of £7000 a year. Its offices are inside those of the NUS. It has just produced a magazine, *Blot*, which is financed by the Gulbenkian Foundation and violently criticized by many teachers. At the moment its policies centre around those issues most immediately popular with its membership, campaigning against school uniform, and caning, and opposing petty rules like forcible eviction into the playground at break times and compulsory games.

If John Munford had his way school would not be compulsory, boring teachers would get few pupils, and many more people from ordinary jobs would take turns teaching in schools. If jobs were available pupils would be able to do some work outside. Adults would be encouraged to come and learn as well, to try to break down the barriers between school and the community.

John Munford believes that under some such free system pupils would be likely to learn more. With coercion removed they would have no need to rebel against being taught. He says that children who hang around the streets all day have a miserable time, for the most part, and would choose to be in school.

I have no idea whether he is right, and children would actually learn more. But I am sure they would be happier. I very much doubt whether they would end up learning less, and we shouldn't have to spend so much time threatening thirteen and fourteen year olds that if they don't eat up their theorems they will end up on the scrap heap.

The Guardian

Keeping his Love

Vera Brittain

Vera Brittain was one of the earliest women to study at Oxford University but she left her studies in 1915 to become a volunteer nurse tending the wounded in the First World War. Her own background was comfortable but she willingly went into the desperate conditions of the field hospitals with their filth and agony. The tragedy of war was a constant theme in her writing. She wrote of the death of her fiancé, of her dearly-loved brother Edward, who was killed by a sniper's bullet, and of the loss of a whole generation of young men in battle.

Apart from her vivid writing about war and her nursing experience, she went on to write fiction, travel and poetry. She is perhaps best remembered for her autobiographical writing, for example *Testament of Youth*, which also shows the development of her interest in social and political issues.

The following article is one of many Vera wrote about the re-balancing of the relationship between men and women which had been much affected by the war and the votes-for-women movement. Although this article was written to better the situation of women, she did not forget that men have a right to be equally respected as human beings.

T he other day my attention was arrested by an article in one of those popular little magazines with coloured covers which are now appearing in such large numbers to tempt the slender purse of the 'home woman'. The article was entitled 'Keeping House for Him', and opened as follows:

> The career of the homeworker is the finest in the world. If you can keep your husband's house efficiently, you can also keep his love ... Every wife is ambitious for her husband, and, when you come to think of it, a lot depends

on her. She has to do with his smart appearance and his punctuality, her cooking makes a great difference to his health, and if she is a cheerful, happy little woman as well as a careful manager, he will be able to go to work free of all home worries.

I can see thousands of 'little women' – to say nothing of their husbands and their critical mothers-in-law – reading over these sugary-sweet sentiments with murmurs of purring approval. Like the writer of the article, they gladly take for granted that, because the work and the objects of the woman-in-the-little-house coincide so exactly with the description here given, they always will and always ought so to coincide. How many of these readers, I wonder, perceive the flagrantly immoral assumptions underlying these childishly innocent paragraphs? Perhaps we can help them to see by a brief analysis.

The first and fundamental assumption made is that a husband, in relation to his wife, is not a rational human being but a peculiarly exacting animal, whose love, which at best is cupboard love, has to be 'kept' by good food, creature comforts, and the same kind of protection against all worries as a too-conscientious mother arranges for her child.

According to assumption number two, a wife is a person without a life of her own. All her activities are second-hand, directed to the career, the appearance, the health, and the punctuality of another person.

Assumption number three impresses upon the 'little woman' that home responsibilities – which include some of the most important problems of life, such as the health and education of children – are not mutual burdens to be lightened for each by being shared with the other. The husband is to be 'spared' them, and the wife, whether competent or not, has to shoulder them all.

Fourthly, the wife is never to be herself, at ease with her husband as one may be at ease with a good, understanding friend. She is always to be acting, pretending to cheerfulness, and concealing difficulties with which her husband has the first right to be acquainted. In other words, throughout her married life she is to play the part of a first-class hypocrite.

Finally, such a marriage can never even approach a happy comradeship based on mutual confidence and respect. It is an employer and employee relation of the worst type, in which the employer is irrational, impatient, unadaptable, and at the mercy of quite unpredictable moods, while the employee receives no wages beyond her keep, and is unprotected by trade union regulations in a most exacting task.

Such assumptions as these, of course, have their origin in our antiquated ideas of courtship – ideas derived from the artificial emotions of the ages of chivalry. These manufactured emotions played their part in the development of human relationships, but their continuance is fatal to that complete honesty of men and women in their dealings with one another which is a main object of the feminist movement and the keystone of the new morality. This dishonesty in the conduct of love dies hard, for we cling as pathetically to the forlorn expedients of insincere artifice as the medieval maiden once clung to her superstitious faith in the love potion. Nothing could prove the struggling survival of the old methods of husband-hunting more clearly than an advertisement, which I came across the other day, in one of the leading American newspapers, of a book designed to coach the would-be wife in the arts of fascination.

> Jane Johns is one girl who felt that she was unattractive to men – but she really did something about it. She actually made a serious study of her most attractive girl friends. She observed thousands of tiny things about them that go to make up their great 'It' – and she practised them until she became the most popular girl in her set. She found that she had more 'It' than she ever dreamed of. Then she studied the men she knew and discovered for herself secrets which every unmarried girl would love to know. In short, she learned the mystery of being attractive.

Whether we are English or American it is surely time that our attitude toward the men with whom we work, the men that we marry, and the men into whom our sons will grow, acquired a dignity which is compatible with our political freedom, our present educational standards, and quite incompatible with the propitiatory, apologetic expediencies of bygone ages. To treat a lover or a husband as though he must be humoured like a naughty child or a pet dog is in reality the expression of a profound contempt both for manhood and for marriage. We have no right to select as a lifelong companion any individual for whom we feel so little respect. Tact is necessary in all personal relationships, but even tact becomes mere despicable manoeuvring unless it is based upon an assumption of reasonableness in the other person.

There is still too wide a belief that the art of wifehood – an art that should be studied before matrimony and not only after it – consists of mollifying a child or propitiating an employer. Actually nothing is further from the ideal expressed in our own marriage service than a mother-and-child or employer-and-employee relation. 'The mutual society, help, and comfort that the one ought to have of the other' implies an agreement entered into by loyal adult companions and based upon an equal love and reverence. Such love and reverence do not grow from protection or propitiation, but from the knowledge that one's partner is a respect-worthy and dignified person. To acquire dignity and reasonableness – that is the major task of every human being, whether male or female. The woman who is conscious of possessing these qualities, and who has wisely chosen her husband because he possesses them too, can safely leave the contemptible little expedients of husband-holding to be practised by the infantile-minded who have failed to understand what is meant by adulthood.

Manchester Guardian, 29 November 1929

Road to Ruin

Gareth Grundy

In this extract Grundy shows us a real place, a once-lovely woodland which meant a great deal to those living nearby. For those who were pro motorway-bypass, there was much to be said for the loss of some trees, for those against, it was a special place, and the writer is sensitive to both attitudes. Will this article speak to later generations as it does to young people in the mid-nineties who buy *The Face* regularly? If care for our environment is vital to those for whom Gareth Grundy writes, will it continue to be for their children or will they look at this article, with its 'language of the day', and see only something quaint and outdated?

April 29, 2.30am, M65 security compound, east side, Stanworth Valley, Lancashire. A dozen men line abreast under halogen lights – miniatures of the sort of thing you find in corners of football stadia. Arms folded, they're doing their best to look fierce and imposing. There's a road protest going on and they've machinery to protect. Directly in front of them, two straggle-haired hippies hammer out a crude rhythm on giant tom-toms, their friends dancing in circles around them. One swigs from a bottle of paraffin, spitting sheets of fire across a lighted branch. Shrieks and yelps come from the woods at the edge of the compound, followed by a dozen men and women. Completely naked. Bar a few nose rings.

Group 4 Security's finest drop their hard hats in utter disbelief. It's difficult to pretend you're big, hard and protecting something more important than Land Rovers when confronted by a bunch of crusties without their clothes on. As protests go, it beats waving placards in Parliament Square. As an attempt to stop further roads being built across our countryside, it may also have been far more effective.

Remember the Ewok village in *Return of the Jedi,* the treetop town populated by spear-chucking teddy bears? Well it existed in Lancashire. Substitute the furry creatures with 60 scruffy hippies, change the film set to Stanworth Valley, throw in 32 tree houses and you're there. A handful of protesters first occupied the valley last August, the first tree house going up that September. By taking up residence high in the trees, the squatters hoped to make themselves harder to evict. Seventy feet above the ground, the homes were constructed from waste wood, tarpaulin and sheer bravery. Sure, the protesters use proper climbing gear, but it's brown trousers time that high up – the tree houses sway in the wind, and you're dangling 70 feet above the Lancashire countryside with only bits of metal and rope between safety and a smashed spine. The only way up is hauling yourself skywards on a harness. Abseiling is the sole way down.

The protesters, however, are up and down like monkeys. Lovingly carpeted, wallpapered with blankets and stocked with supplies, some of the tree houses are even divided into rooms, one above the other. And if you want to visit your neighbour? You use the 'walkways' – two blue polypropylene ropes linking tree to tree, fanning out through the valley's canopy in an azure spider's web. One rope's for your hands and the other is for standing on. Hook your climbing harness to the top rope in case you fall, and you're away.

Liz has been living up a tree since January, alongside a hardcore of about 50 protesters who stuck out a snowy Lancashire winter. Articulate, opinionated and passionate about road protests, she's one of the figures the Stanworth community looks to for leadership. Until last summer she was a Management Studies student in Manchester; now she says that understanding how institutions work helps her protesting. Liz was involved in the opposition to the M11 in Wanstead while still at college, but this is her first full-on action. 'Before I came here I could barely bang a nail in straight,' she says. 'Now I'm living in a house I built myself. Living in the trees has given me a sense of freedom.'

Protesters use walkways to cross from tree to tree

It's strange that the lure of tarmac should provide the focus to create an entire community. Traveller culture might have saddled us with The Levellers and white kids with really bad dreads, but it also birthed a new form of eco-oriented direct action in which marches were replaced by occupation and non-violent physical defence of greenery under threat. Since the M3 rolled through Twyford Down in 1992, the major flashpoints have been Solsbury Hill in 1994, last year's face-off on the M11 at Wanstead, and this year's action over the M77 at Pollock. The M65 campaign is the most imaginative yet.

Replacing beech with bitumen will extend the M65 by thirteen miles, linking Blackburn to Burnley. Both places are the grey colour of post-industrial Britain, sorely in need of any greenery they possess. The extension, backed by a £20 million business development plan with cross-party support, ends a scheme to link east Lancashire to Britain's major road network, first unveiled in 1937. Stanworth Valley lies directly in its path.

It's a beautiful place, with freakish geographics. About a mile in circumference, its sides are so steep it's like a huge bowl – filled with giant trees, and with the River Hoddlesworth running across its floor. In winter, Stanworth is knee-deep in mud, but spring leaves it carpeted with bluebells. Locals from the nearby village of Fensicowles use it regularly – families on Sunday afternoon walks, or the ubiquitous Kid On Mountain Bike. Many of them follow the disused canal running along the valley's northern rim. A derelict railway marks out the valley's southern edge. Now Stanworth is set for the only land-based form of mass transport it's missed out on. The car. To be precise it's getting a 'viaduct', a six-lane concrete flyover running east to west, and brutally cleaving the valley in two.

'The real story is about the community here,' says Flynn, a bearded Scouse motormouth and Liz's boyfriend. 'It's about people coming together, about the basics – food, warmth, shelter. There's all sorts of people here – students, drop-outs, whoever. It doesn't matter. If you're cold and wet and somebody builds a fire or hands you a mug of tea, that's what matters. That binds us as much as the road. People ask how we can live here like this. I just say we've got no negative equity. We don't own anything, so we've got nothing stressing us out.'

A full-time traveller, Flynn lives in a caravan at a paper mill near the valley – the protesters' own Checkpoint Charlie. Like many here, he was at Twyford and Wanstead, and like many he's ambivalent about press attention: fear of the DSS and police mean names and ages aren't readily doled out. Despite this, I like Flynn, and not just because he let me sleep a night in his warm caravan. With a definite gift of the gab, he's one of those people who could talk his way into anything, but mostly into trouble. Sometimes he takes his traveller mates back to the Wirral to meet his dad, who's a policeman. 'He's really into us,' laughs Flynn.

Despite the dogs and screeching penny whistles, the Stanworth community defies the crusty stereotype. They're not weekend dread-wearers, up for a rant at anyone in uniform, nor the cider-swigging soft crusties that overran the nation's campuses a couple of years back. Their commitment and knowledge is beyond doubt.

'You talk to some people in Blackburn,' says Liz, 'and they'll be in favour of the road, because they think it'll bring jobs. But what sort of jobs? In motorway service stations? And how long will they be there? There's loads more that can be done in this area. There's a huge landfill that needs cleaning up for a start. You need to localize the economy. I ask people if they've got children, and whether any of those children have asthma or not. Then I ask them what they think about pollution.'

* * *

They might have opted out of conventional society, but some things the normal world does badly, the Stanworth protesters do very well – like taking care of each other. There's always a fire built if someone's cold, food if someone's hungry, tea and sympathy if there's tears.

However, they do buy into some of modern society's more useful toys. Like the mobile phone. Liz has one, and a solar panel to recharge the battery, for co-ordinating the protest. Grant, a cheery, mohawked Scot with a withered left arm, owns one too. But this was harder to come by. 'You need a credit rating and a permanent address to get one, don't you?' he chuckles. 'I had to give them me mum's. You see, you can't get a mobile if you're a mobile person.'

March 27, midday, M65 security compound, Stanworth Valley, western slope. A yellow, dirt-flecked bulldozer sits motionless in the mud, engine silent, its driver flicking through *The Sun*. His charge can't go anywhere because it's sprinkled with crusties, wedging themselves between the hydraulics and underneath caterpillar tracks. A Land Rover draws up, and eight or ten mustachioed security men bound down the slope as fast as their beer-guts allow. Amid screams of protest, they manhandle people off the machine, herding them back towards the valley.

Since they're obliged to use only minimum force, this takes time, requiring at least two beer bellies to remove one protester. Before retreating, the protesters form a circle, performing an incongruous, impromptu Ring-A-Roses. Not for nothing do they regard their protest as 'fluffy' – at times it's naive and childlike. The security men look on, scratching their heads. 'Well, they believe in it, don't they?' says one, refusing to give his name. 'So you have to respect that. No way would you get me up in those trees! I don't see how they're gonna stop anything though. But then I don't see how they're gonna get them down from the trees, either.'

Employed by the construction companies building the M65 extension, Amec and McAlpine, to protect their sites, Group 4 and their ilk have no power to remove protesters from the valley. They're there – round the clock – to stop sabotage and pick up overtime cheques.

Also prominent in the March actions against diggers is Lai, a 23-year-old Malaysian and student in Philosophy and Politics in London. 'At first, for me, this protest was about the road,' he explains. 'Now it's symbolic of all British woodland. I love greenery, but you can't go anywhere in this country without a big road near it. I looked at the map the other day and I managed to find somewhere: Salisbury

Plain. Then a friend said, 'You can't go there. The army owns it. They use it to blow up tanks!'

After an initially wary period, the majority of Fensicowles' residents are models of tolerance. Its bored teenage population think the protesters are the best thing since Sega, and they trek to the woods to sit around fires, sharing underage drink and dope. The protest has put the village on the map and reminded many inhabitants they don't want the road either. Some donate food to the protesters, others offer baths. You'll find a few who think they're a bunch of layabout outsiders, and there were rumours that protesters were banned from one village pub, The Fieldens Arms. Enquiries at the bar meet with a predictable 'dunno mate', but one of the customers, Joe Ferguson, proved more talkative.

'I used to do a bit of protesting myself in my younger days,' he says. 'Ban The Bomb, that sort of thing, and I took a few cracks over the head from the police. Most people here are behind the tree people. They've stuck it out and it's a peaceful protest. Most of us work, so we don't have time or can't afford to join in. They're a mouthpiece for the rest of us. The roads here are murder, so maybe we need something doing. But I don't think the M65 is it.'

April 26. Months of High Court wrangling over the occupation of Stanworth Valley ends. Unsurprisingly, the protest is deemed illegal and the squatters will now be evicted. Two days later, protesters meet the man charged with turfing them out, the Under Sheriff of Lancashire, Andrew Wilson, to discuss safety. Wilson, also a solicitor, is Secretary of the National Under Sheriffs Association. Outwardly amenable, in the manner of your average crocodile-smiling MP, he stresses he doesn't want any trouble, and safety will be paramount. He is, after all, just doing a job. The protesters tell the sheriff there won't be any 'violent' resistance, and take his statements about safety as promises of non-aggression on the part of his bailiffs. Both sides come away reassured. The task of prising people from branches 70 feet up remains.

April 30. Stanworth Valley crackles with excitement, nervous over the next morning's expected eviction. More protesters arrive, swelling their number to about 100, half on the ground, half in the air. Today is also Beltane, the pagan celebration of the end of April. The resulting celebration hastens the spiralling tensions – the air is thick with the sound of drums and penny whistles. As part of the fun, there's a communal fire down by the river, with a ritual burning of a wicker man and a sweat lodge – a sauna built from branches and blankets and filled with stones from the fire. Protesters undress and sit inside. When they're hot and sweaty enough, they rush into the river to cool down. Then of course, it's off to see the boys from Group 4, which is where we came in.

At about three in the morning, the nipple ring flaunting over, I bump into Liz at the bottom of her tree. She's been hiding most of the weekend, consumed by the stress of eviction preparations. Things aren't getting any easier. A local woman has just phoned her to say that her husband has left her and their kids to join the protesters. She just thought Liz ought to know. Liz takes it personally. 'I just burst into tears,' she sighs. On top of that she's got a TV company trying to persuade her to do a video diary of the eviction.

May 1, 8am. Over 200 police, with a similar number of private security staff in tow, march into Stanworth from the east. They seal off a 'sterile area', blue tape on the ground mirroring the rope draped through the trees. Anyone on the ground within the tape must leave, or they'll be escorted out, anyone returning will be arrested. The tree dwellers quickly scamper up their respective trunks, assuming defensive positions along the walkways. The national media turn up too, identifiable by fresh Gore-tex and that other outdoor staple, the cashmere overcoat. Ever helpful, the police have marked out a press pen, by the Group 4 compound on the edge of the valley. Few bother to leave it during the eviction.

Sheriff Wilson's masterplan – use a team of half-a-dozen expert climbers and it'll all be over in time for tea – fails miserably. It's a ludicrous underestimation of the opposition. These people are defending what they regard as home, so naturally the climbers' attempts to grab hold of them are met with physical brush-offs.

The 'fluffiness', it seems, is over. The climbers – variously rumoured to be mountain rescue or tree surgeons, although no one would confirm which – have had enough. Bailiffs now ride shotgun with them. Protesters are chased along walkways in a dangerous game of high-wire cat and mouse, arms and legs lashing out from both sides. The first tree houses fall, ripped apart and thrown to the ground. Actions on both sides become increasingly fraught. Worryingly, the bailiffs carry knives to cut ropes with. Fine, it's their job, but you'd feel safer if they could actually climb. One makes it up a tree, only to realize he can't descend as he's never been taught to abseil. A climber has to tell him what to do.

By the second day, walkways are being cut with people on them and handcuffs used on unruly protesters, leaving them helpless up high. By chainsawing the trees behind the bailiffs, space is made to bring in cherry pickers – large hydraulic arms with baskets on the end – making the job quicker and easier. Food and water is hurled at climbers, the debris hitting the police video camera here to 'record events'. I try my best to smile when it's pointed at me.

The defence of Stanworth Valley soon falters in the face of the Sheriff's overwhelming resources, although the Sheriff himself has to return to his offices in Preston at one point to deal with a sit-in from unhappy protesters. By Friday May 5, it's all over. The world's only life-size replica of a George Lucas set has been destroyed. And a broad, ugly, tree-free strip of mud runs through the middle of the valley.

'I'm doing the accounts at the moment,' says Sheriff Wilson. 'It's been a very expensive exercise.' The M65 project has cost £145 million. Prior to the eviction, the bill for security was £2.2 million. There were 61 arrests, mostly for interfering with a lawful activity, i.e. the eviction.

Understandably, the protesters were miffed with Wilson, due to what they regarded as violence by the bailiffs. 'The bailiffs were used because the tree climbers were having the hell kicked out of them,' insists the Sheriff.

'I was dismayed with the sort of resistance we met, resistance that was, in the view of myself and the police, violent. And yes, I think the climbers worked very well with the bailiffs.'

Weren't you amazed that no one was seriously injured? 'Well, I've said before that if this kind of protest continues, then someone is going to get killed. It was a deliberate decision to cut the walkways. Certainly the risk was there and I never pretended otherwise. I was underneath them and none were cut in any situation in which I thought anyone was in danger. But we had to show this was not a game of tag in the trees. We had a court order to enforce. What did they expect me to do? Starve them out? Some protesters occupied my garden on Wednesday [May 10]. That seems most unnecessary. The only person at home was my mother, who's 78 years old. That is going beyond legitimate protest.'

You could start your own small country on the cost of road protesting. The bill for the M11 eviction weighed in at £14 million, upping the road's budget by 38 per cent. Early this May, the Government failed to sue 76 protesters over the £1.9 million cost of the Twyford Down actions. In the meantime, ten Twyford protesters have won £50,000 in damages for wrongful arrest, with 40 more cases pending. Eleven M11 protesters are still being sued.

Despite the eviction, the relatively small number of Stanworth protesters achieved their aims – publicity for their cause (fewer roads, better public transport), the delay of this road, and the message that future roads planned through environmentally-sensitive areas will have the additional cost of protests weighed against them. But a community that lived, loved and dodged the cops together rose and fell in the process.

Their tree-clambering antics make them both a bunch of crazy crusties and some of the bravest people you'll ever meet. While their contemporaries dance their fear away on pharmaceuticals and a 4/4 beat, it's good to find folks with such a strong sense of belief. They like their cigarettes and alcohol as much as anyone, it's just that their choice of rebellion has an end. Who knows if it's achievable, but at least they're trying.

'My dad saw me and Flynn on telly when we were at Wanstead,' says one of them, Noel, softly from behind his Lennon specs. 'We were charging this line of policemen. He said it was the proudest moment of his life.'

The Face

The English Riot

Neil Ascherson

Neil Ascherson has written a regular column for *The Observer* for several years. He challenges traditional ideas about what it means to be British and examines closely some of our less attractive behaviour. In the article below, written in 1985, he reflects on the long history of rioting as a feature of British life. He points out that desperation has fuelled rioting amongst those who can see no other way of bringing attention to their plight. He looks at the situation of the police force positioned between the law-abiding citizens and the law-breakers. In doing so, although you may perceive where his sympathies lie, you can see that he gives space to both the rioters' reasons for rioting and the strain the law-enforcers come under. In his own introduction to *Games with Shadows*, the book in which this article was also published, he explains that writing his regular column was an 'attempt to find out what I did believe about the world in which I lived'.

After a great riot, there is much to be cleared away: the rubble, the burned-out cars, the broken glass, But then, for weeks afterwards, there is work to do clearing away the thick layer of nonsense which sifts down like ash from the stratosphere upon us all.

It is familiar nonsense. We hear that the fearful events at Brixton and Broadwater Farm were 'mere criminality,' that they were instigated by professional agitators (the old 'stormy petrel' theory which has attended every disturbance for centuries). We hear that it was all the fault of the police or, conversely, the natural consequence of harbouring an alien, 'ungovernable' race in British cities. We hear the tragic, understandable cry of a policeman: 'This isn't England!'

But it is. Rioting is at least as English as thatched cottages and honey still for tea. It is right to be appalled when young men – black and white together – burn, loot and rape and fight the police with petrol bombs, knives and guns. But it is badly wrong to conclude that we are entering unknown territory, that a violent break has been made with some 'law-abiding', gentle past of plebeian Britain to which intellectuals like Orwell, Leavis, even T S Eliot, used to appeal.

Before the organization of a proper police force, there were countless popular explosions, from the Gordon riots of 1780 which left over 200 dead in London to upheavals like the Reform riots in Bristol in 1831. People spoke then about 'the dangerous classes', about 'human vermin' and 'moral sewage'. The London police were first issued with firearms in 1883, when 821 officers received training in their use. There was Luddism, the 'Captain Swing' movement in the countryside, the Rebecca riots in rural Wales.

But in 'modern times', within living memory, the tradition has persisted. This country was torn by violence in 1919, for example. First came the race riots against black seamen, which flared around all the major sea-ports. Then came the outbreak in Luton, when crowds burned the town hall with petrol; there were over 100 casualties and troops had to be brought in. The next month, the police went on strike in Liverpool, and there followed days and nights of fighting and looting, put down by troops who had to charge with the bayonet while tanks moved into the Scotland Road area. All through that summer, crowds of young people challenged and fought the police in London – in Brixton, Tottenham and Wood Green, among other places.

There were unemployed riots in 1921, and much bigger outbreaks in 1931. In Manchester, the Army was called out in support of the civil power, and the police used high-pressure hoses against the mobs. In Glasgow, the police attacked a demonstration of 50,000 people on Glasgow Green, precipitating a huge riot in which there was widespread looting and the storming of defended tenement blocks.

Behind these full-scale riots, potential violence simmered permanently in the poorest quarters of the cities. This was thought deplorable, but not a cause for panic. Sir Robert Mark, in his memoirs, remembers violent street battles in Manchester as he – then a plain copper on the beat – went in for an arrest. But to him there was something 'cheerful' about it. In such tumults, accompanied by drunkenness and looting at times, ' a good time was had by all'.

Rioting, in short, is one of the instruments of British political behaviour. It is a terrifying instrument, not often used, but it is the traditional resort of those who feel excluded and oppressed by the social and political structure under which – rather than in which – they live.

Home Secretaries, by the nature of their job, are almost bound to overlook this. Douglas Hurd predictably said that all the riots were 'the result of criminal action', but – as he observed in a striking interview the other day – he is emphatically not a Minister of the Interior. He does not 'command' law and order or tell the police what to do; his job is not much more than mediating between the needs of the police and prison services and the wishes of the Government.

The nation turns to him for the first comment after a riot, but in fact he is only able to mention the problems it sets the police. Unless the Prime Minister chooses to utter, everything about a riot except its 'criminality' aspect will be ignored.

I remember, a dozen years ago, meeting Sir Robert Mark in an Oxford college. Just as I joined the group around him, he was completing a thought. I caught only the last sentence which has, none the less, always stayed in my mind. He said: 'You will see in the next few years that the police will be recognized as the most important social service.'

An indefinable chill settled on me. On the face of it, this was a liberal thing to say: a promise of a new, caring gendarmerie whose task would be not only to repress the villain but to organize youth clubs, tend the single parent, suggest beneficial hobbies to the unemployed. For the Home Office, read the Ministry of Love. And, indeed, Sir Robert's thought has now issued in the ideal of 'community policing' and other hopeful projects.

I don't want to insult all this effort when I say that the Old Bill remains the Old Bill, and the policeman's lot is happier when he accepts that. The police is for enforcing law and order. It is not for alleviating the conditions which give rise to crime, a job for politicians. One of the nastiest features of Mrs Thatcher's Government has been to abandon whole regions of social responsibility and dump the consequences on the police. The miners' strike was one example, and the White Paper on Public Order (offering police commanders essentially political powers over demonstrations) was another.

The 'police as social service' is interventionist. You go into bad areas, you poke about with good intentions, you come on naughty activities and then you have to do something about them. Much trouble has been avoided in the past by leaving 'the dangerous classes' alone in their burrows as far as possible; one thinks of 'Campbell Bunk', that lawless antheap of old north London, which the police only raided when disorder approached the civil war level. Ferreting about for suspects, let alone frightening ladies into heart attacks or shooting them, would have detonated Campbell Bunk like an ammunition dump.

Much has been written about the history of British rioting. It tends to show that rioters are not all 'scum' or 'criminals', and that they often have quite a clear idea about why they did what they did. After the fearsome disorders in Watts, California, in 1965, the blacks described their action as a 'revolt' and believed that good would come of it. The mood in Broadwater Farm, even after the atrocious killing of PC Blakelock, is one of defiant pride. They see the police (wrongly) as their enemy: now at last they have fought the enemy, and nothing will ever be the same.

The last word can stay with Jerry White, a contributor to *New Society* just after the inner-city outbreaks of 1981. He wrote: 'Riot has classically been a collective weapon of the politically powerless – to get those with power and wealth to share a little more and to take notice; to effect revenge; and to preserve traditions and rights from attack'.

Activities

The activities which follow might be used for discussion or written tasks.

A War: Edward Bawden, Mary Seacole, John Smith, Anne Frank, Zlata Filipovic and Neil Ascherson

War features several times in the extracts in this book. Use two or more of the extracts and show how war affects the lives and places that the writers describe. What views of war do these writers have? Try to say what these are and how far they agree with your own views.

B Swapping genres: Mary Seacole and Bob Geldof

1 Read the extract from *Wonderful Adventures of Mary Seacole in Many Lands.* Recast her writing as diary entries over several days. Bear in mind that Mary Seacole wrote her autobiography for the public to read, and that a private diary kept over these days might have a different and more personal tone. Look back at some of the personal diary and journal writing in this book to give you ideas.

2 Read the extract from Bob Geldof's autobiography *Is That It?* and think about the way the release of the song 'Do They Know It's Christmas?' would have appeared to people at the time. Write an article for a daily newspaper the day after the song reached Number One. Decide whether you are writing for a tabloid or broadsheet paper. Combine real facts with your own opinions.

C Replying to Sarah

Read *Sarah's Letters.*

1 Write a reply to Sarah as if you were her English teacher, Dr Harrison. Remember that you are in role as a teacher when writing to her; you do know her quite well but you need to remain objective yet encouraging.

2 Write a reply to Sarah as yourself, having read her letter published in this book. Imagine being able to give her some advice and encouragement which could help her through her shyness and unhappiness in school.

D Conversations across the years:
1 Anne Frank meets Zlata Filipovic OR
2 Amelia Edwards meets Christina Dodwell

1 Read the extracts from Anne Frank's and Zlata Filipovik's diaries. Write the script for a conversation between Anne and Zlata. Remember that they were schoolgirl writers, whose family and friends were important to them. They would share a common experience of war and of being shut away, although Anne's hiding-place protected her from betrayal rather than military attack.

2 Read the extracts from *A Thousand Miles up the Nile* by Amelia Edwards and *A Traveller in China* by Christina Dodwell. Imagine these two travellers meeting. Write a script for a conversation between them in which they talk about the journeys they each made. They would be likely to ask each other about the differences between their ways of travelling. You might try to keep the speech in the style of the original writing.

E Looking at persuasive language: Vera Brittain and Gareth Grundy

Look back at the articles by Brittain and Grundy.

1 Grundy calls the protesters 'straggle-haired hippies' and security men 'beer bellies'. Does his choice of language show him siding with one or the other side?

2 Using the examples above and examples from other journalism, write about the way language can be used to persuade readers either to take the writer's point of view or to weigh up the evidence for themselves. Whose 'side' do you find yourself on as you read? Bear in mind that the writer has a viewpoint but is also presenting other people for your approval or disapproval.

F Taking the law into their own hands: Polly Toynbee, Neil Ascherson and Gareth Grundy

Journalists often question the way society works. Toynbee suggests adolescents might give up school, Ascherson suggests that rioters believe they might correct injustice by actively law-breaking, Grundy shows other protesters peacefully blocking motorway plans.

1 Take two real-life examples in which people have gone against the law, either using the examples in this book, or other examples with which you are familiar. Write about both examples, showing more than one point of view in each case.

2 Come to your own conclusion about whether it can be right to break the law sometimes.

G Re-grouping the extracts

The extracts in this book have been grouped under five genre headings:

Diaries and journals

Biography and autobiography

Letters

Travel

People's ideas

Several of the extracts could be grouped under more than one genre heading. Imaging you are the editor of this book and wish to make a new arrangement of the extracts. Consider the features of the writing in each genre and then make a different grouping of the extracts under these five headings. Write a report explaining how you have arrived at this re-arrangement.

Acknowledgements

The Publishers should like to thank the following for permission to use photographs/copyright material:

The Anne Frank Foundation for the extracts from *The Diary of Anne Frank*, © copyright 1952 by Otto H Frank Basel/ANNE FRANK-Fonds Basel/Switzerland, p2; Penguin Group for the extracts from *Zlata's Diary* by Zlata Filipovic, translated by Christina Pribichevich-Zorich, Viking 1994, p15; John Smith for the extracts from *74 Days: An Islander's Diary of the Falklands Occupation* by John Smith, Century Publishing 1984, p22; Frederick Warne & Co. for the extract from *The Journal of Beatrix Potter 1881–1897* by Beatrix Potter, Frederick Warne & Co. 1966, p29; The Estate of Francis Kilvert for the extracts from *Kilvert's Diary: Selections from the Diary of Rev. Francis Kilvert 1870–1879* by Francis Kilvert, (ed.) William Plomer, Jonathan Cape 1944, p34; Macmillan Publishers Ltd for the extract from *Is That It?* by Bob Geldof, Sidgwick and Jackson 1986, p40; Frank Graham for the extracts from *A Lang Way to the Panshop* by Thomas Callaghan, Publisher Frank Graham, p48; Falling Wall Press for the extract from *The Wonderful Adventures of Mrs Seacole in Many Lands* by Mary Seacole, Falling Wall Press 1984, p54; Little, Brown & Co. for the extract from *The Long Walk to Freedom: the Autobiography of Nelson Mandela* by Nelson Mandela, Little Brown & Co. 1994, p64; Dr Bernard T Harrison, Sarah, and the Institute of Education, University of London, for the extracts from *Sarah's Letters: A Case of Shyness* by Bernard T Harrison (now Professor and Dean in the Faculty of Education, Edith Cowan University, Perth, Western Australia, and 'Sarah' has recently become a mature entrant into a teaching career), p74; Scolar Press and the Imperial War Museum for the extracts from *Edward Bawden: War Artist and his Letters Home 1940–45* (ed.) Ruari McLean, Scolar Press in association with the Imperial War Museum 1989, p93; Orion Publishing for the extract from *On Foot through Africa* by Ffyona Campbell, Orion Publishing Group Ltd 1995, p100; Harper Collins *Publishers* Ltd for the extract from *A Short Walk in the*

Hindu Kush by Eric Newby, Secker & Warburg 1958, p109; Hodder & Stoughton Ltd for the extract from *A Traveller in China* by Christina Dodwell, Hodder & Stoughton 1985, p117; Constable & Co. Ltd for the extract from *Journey through Europe* by John Hillaby, Granada Publishing 1978, p125; Thomas Nelson and Sons Ltd for 'Examinations' by Polly Toynbee in *Varieties of Writing* (eds) J Brown and D Jackson, Macmillan Education Ltd 1984, p140; Vera Brittain's article 'Keeping his Love' from *Testament of a Generation* is included with the permission of Paul Berry, her Literary Executor, p144; Gareth Grundy for 'Road to Ruin' from *The Face* No 82 July 1985, p148; Peters Fraser & Dunlop Ltd for the extracts from *The English Riot* by Neil Ascherson, Century Hutchinson 1988, p159.

The Publishers have made every effort to trace the copyright holders, but if they have inadvertently overlooked any, they will be pleased to make the necessary arrangements at the first opportunity.

Photographs
© Paul Lowe/Magnum, p14; © Frank Spooner Pictures/ Gamma, p25; Mansell Collection, p55; © Institute of Education, University of London, p80; © Christina Dodwell p119; Tim Ockenden/Press Association/Topham, p150.

HEINEMANN NEW WINDMILLS

Founding Editors: Anne and Ian Serraillier

Chinua Achebe Things Fall Apart
Vivien Alcock The Cuckoo Sister; The Monster Garden;
The Trial of Anna Cotman; A Kind of Thief; Ghostly Companions
Margaret Atwood The Handmaid's Tale
Jane Austen Pride and Prejudice
J G Ballard Empire of the Sun
Nina Bawden The Witch's Daughter; A Handful of Thieves; Carrie's
War; The Robbers; Devil by the Sea; Kept in the Dark; The Finding;
Keeping Henry; Humbug; The Outside Child
Valerie Bierman No More School
Melvin Burgess An Angel for May
Ray Bradbury The Golden Apples of the Sun; The Illustrated Man
Betsy Byars The Midnight Fox; Goodbye, Chicken Little; The
Pinballs; The Not-Just-Anybody Family; The Eighteenth Emergency
Victor Canning The Runaways; Flight of the Grey Goose
Ann Coburn Welcome to the Real World
Hannah Cole Bring in the Spring
Jane Leslie Conly Racso and the Rats of NIMH
Robert Cormier We All Fall Down; Tunes for Bears to Dance to
Roald Dahl Danny, The Champion of the World; The Wonderful
Story of Henry Sugar; George's Marvellous Medicine; The BFG;
The Witches; Boy; Going Solo; Matilda
Anita Desai The Village by the Sea
Charles Dickens A Christmas Carol; Great Expectations;
Hard Times; Oliver Twist; A Charles Dickens Selection
Peter Dickinson Merlin Dreams
Berlie Doherty Granny was a Buffer Girl; Street Child
Roddy Doyle Paddy Clarke Ha Ha Ha
Gerald Durrell My Family and Other Animals
Anne Fine The Granny Project
Anne Frank The Diary of Anne Frank
Leon Garfield Six Apprentices; Six Shakespeare Stories;
Six More Shakespeare Stories
Jamila Gavin The Wheel of Surya
Adele Geras Snapshots of Paradise

Alan Gibbons Chicken
Graham Greene The Third Man and The Fallen Idol; Brighton Rock
Thomas Hardy The Withered Arm and Other Wessex Tales
L P Hartley The Go-Between
Ernest Hemmingway The Old Man and the Sea; A Farewell to Arms
Nigel Hinton Getting Free; Buddy; Buddy's Song
Anne Holm I Am David
Janni Howker Badger on the Barge; Isaac Campion; Martin Farrell
Jennifer Johnston Shadows on Our Skin
Toeckey Jones Go Well, Stay Well
Geraldine Kaye Comfort Herself; A Breath of Fresh Air
Clive King Me and My Million
Dick King-Smith The Sheep-Pig
Daniel Keyes Flowers for Algernon
Elizabeth Laird Red Sky in the Morning; Kiss the Dust
D H Lawrence The Fox and The Virgin and the Gypsy;
Selected Tales
Harper Lee To Kill a Mockingbird
Ursula Le Guin A Wizard of Earthsea
Julius Lester Basketball Game
C Day Lewis The Otterbury Incident
David Line Run for Your Life
Joan Lingard Across the Barricades; Into Exile; The Clearance;
The File on Fraulein Berg
Robin Lister The Odyssey
Penelope Lively The Ghost of Thomas Kempe
Jack London The Call of the Wild; White Fang
Bernard Mac Laverty Cal; The Best of Bernard Mac Laverty
Margaret Mahy The Haunting
Jan Mark Do You Read Me? (Eight Short Stories)
James Vance Marshall Walkabout
W Somerset Maughan The Kite and Other Stories
Ian McEwan The Daydreamer; A Child in Time
Pat Moon The Spying Game
Michael Morpurgo Waiting for Anya; My Friend Walter;
The War of Jenkins' Ear
Bill Naughton The Goalkeeper's Revenge
New Windmill A Charles Dickens Selection
New Windmill Book of Classic Short Stories
New Windmill Book of Nineteenth Century Short Stories

How many have you read?